Every Day with
Jesus

JUL/AUG 2022

Copyright © Waverley Abbey Resources 2022. Published by Waverley Abbey Resources, an operating name of CWR, Waverley Abbey House, Waverley Lane, Farnham, Surrey GU9 8EP, UK. Tel: 01252 784700 Email: mail@waverleyabbey.org

Registered Charity No. 294387. Registered Limited Company No. 1990308.

Front cover image: Adobe Stock Images

Concept development, editing, design and production by Waverley Abbey Resources. Printed in England by Yeomans. All rights reserved. No part of this publication may be reproduced, stored in a retrieval system, or transmitted, in any form or by any means, electronic, mechanical, photocopying, recording or otherwise, without the prior permission in writing of Waverley Abbey Resources.

Unless otherwise indicated, all Scripture references are from the Holy Bible, New International Version® Anglicised, NIV® Copyright © 1979, 1984, 2011 by Biblica, Inc.® Used by permission. All rights reserved worldwide. Scripture taken from the New King James Version®. Copyright © 1982 by Thomas Nelson. Used by permission. All rights reserved.

WAVERLEY ABBEY
RESOURCES

MIX
Paper from
responsible sources
FSC® C021017
www.fsc.org

Every Day with Jesus is available in large print from Waverley Abbey Resources. It is also available on **audio** and **DAISY** in the UK and Eire for the sole use of those with a visual impairment worse than N12, or who are registered blind. For details please contact **Torch Trust for the Blind**, Tel: 01858 438260. Torch House, Torch Way, Northampton Road, Market Harborough LE16 9HL.

Acts 20:32–36

'You yourselves know that these hands of mine have supplied my own needs and the needs of my companions. In everything I did, I showed you that by this kind of hard work we must help the weak, remembering the words the Lord Jesus himself said: "It is more blessed to give than to receive."' (vv34–35)

Serving God and others is the heartbeat of Christian discipleship (Mark 12:29–31). In *EDWJ* we shall explore what this means as we seek to make a God-shaped difference in the world. Paul's clear: we're to take personal responsibility for ourselves, but not at the expense of living in mutual support with others, i.e. community. God's given us everything and encourages us to rely on His grace moment by moment. Paul confirms his needs have been met, even if at times he experienced apparent poverty and risk (Phil. 4:12). Determining our values, our underlying ideals, provide the primary motivators that drive our decisions and focus our life goals. As we set out, I would like us all to adopt Paul's statement, 'It is more blessed to give than to receive', repeating Jesus' own instruction (Luke 6:38). The 2021 Edelman Trust Barometer, an annual, global report, revealed that the world had entered 'a new era of information bankruptcy and a trust ecosystem unable to confront it' after conducting more than 33,000 online surveys in 28 countries in 2020.* If trust is lost, the freedoms we appreciate also disappear, and society struggles to function. God invites us to live by our word, to practise integrity in every situation, even when it appears to discriminate against us. Taking Jesus at His word will prove challenging; however if we cannot, then we face the serious question, what trust can we place in God and Scripture?

SCRIPTURE TO CONSIDER: Deut. 16:13–17; Mal. 3:6–12; 2 Cor. 8:1–9; Heb. 13:1–8.

AN ACTION TO TAKE: Serving can appear challenging because it puts other people first. Do you see this attitude in the life of Jesus? What stories illustrate this?

A PRAYER TO MAKE: 'Lord, encourage me through the life of Jesus to be eager to serve rather than to be served. Amen.'

* edwj.org/ja22-1jul [Accessed 2022/02/18]

Ephesians 4:11–13

'To equip his people for works of service, so that the body of Christ may be built up until we all reach unity in the faith and in the knowledge of the Son of God and become mature, attaining to the whole measure of the fullness of Christ.' (vv12–13)

The word 'service' leads us to acknowledge that we are actually God's servants on earth. Our model is Jesus, who came not to be served, but to serve (Matt. 20:28). This is challenging; seldom will we instinctively seek to become the least amongst our peers. This is not to be mistaken for being a victim or embracing low self-esteem. In fact, quite the opposite, for in God's kingdom the least amongst us is the greatest (Luke 9:48). This is at odds with innumerable reality TV shows that seek to project individuals into the public arena to enjoy their fifteen minutes of fame, a phrase attributed to Andy Warhol, and which he claimed had come true with the rise of celebrity culture in the seventies.* In contrast, Jesus was the child of an unknown virgin, and grew up in Nazareth, an unremarkable village four miles from Galilee's capital, Sepphoris. His birth was in a cowshed, He began life as a refugee, and He frequently requested that the supernatural signs that accompanied His ministry were kept quiet (Luke 5:14). The unremarkable background story of a servant, appreciated by God, even if executed on Jerusalem's rubbish dump beyond the city walls. While many chase self-realisation with the mistaken idea that this will provide happiness and fulfilment, in equipping God's people for acts of service we are to concentrate on helping them discover the art of unremarkable service so that the remarkable generosity of God might shine through and offer a compelling witness to the gospel.

SCRIPTURE TO CONSIDER: Gen. 32:9–32; 1 Sam. 16:4–13; Luke 22:24–30; 1 Cor. 15:1–11.

AN ACTION TO TAKE: What does it take actively to live as the willing servant of all? How can we cultivate a humble heart and disposition?

A PRAYER TO MAKE: 'Lord, may I recognise each day that I am least amongst the people of God. Amen.'

* edwj.org/ja22-2jul [accessed 2022/02/18]

Ephesians 4:14–16
'Then we will no longer be infants, tossed back and forth by the waves, and blown here and there by every wind of teaching and by the cunning and craftiness of people in their deceitful scheming.' (v14)

The objective of moving from childhood to adulthood is maturity – the ability to take care of ourselves and prove productive in the world. Parents miss young adults leaving home, yet were their children to prove incapable of departing, it would be tragic. We all have the ability to mature through learning and experience, both physically and spiritually. There are innumerable perils that seek to shipwreck our Christian faith, and it takes personal resolve and active learning to discover what is true about God's way of living life, and how we might be best equipped to serve God's world. Waverley Abbey was born out of a vision to equip people to live the Christian life effectively. First came *EDWJ*, conceived and written by Selwyn Hughes, founder of Committed to World Revival. These notes were to help people, as they continue to do, to take Bible truth and live it every day. Later, Waverley Abbey House was purchased through the prayer and donations of those committed to strengthening God's witness, and learning was extended to include courses exploring how Christians might become 'people helpers', and so practically love their neighbour. Today, we're expanding that vision beyond Waverley and increasing our online learning to train people globally in practical skills, as well as build on our existing degree courses. Indeed, our ambition is to realise Selwyn's vision and establish a Christian university, with our own degree-awarding powers. As such we will equip generations of Christians in their working life, or as volunteers, to bring the very highest standards to their chosen profession.

SCRIPTURE TO CONSIDER: Ps. 32:8–11; Isa. 54:11–17; Luke 2:41–52; Heb. 6:1–12.

AN ACTION TO TAKE: Would you benefit from developing your skill set? Visit edwj.org/ja22-3jul for more details of our learning programmes.

A PRAYER TO MAKE: 'Lord, I want to learn to be as effective as possible in serving God with my life. Amen.'

The *Cover to Cover* Bible Study Series

Is your church looking for studies this September?

Experience the reality of Bible events like never before and live through the inspiring lives of key characters in Scripture.

Learn how to apply God's Word to your life as you explore seven compelling sessions and gain a new depth in your Bible knowledge.

For more information please visit our website:

wvly.org/c2c

> Deuteronomy 6:4–9
> 'Hear, O Israel: The LORD our God, the LORD is one. Love the LORD your God with all your heart and with all your soul and with all your strength. These commandments that I give you today are to be on your hearts.' (vv4–6)

A podcast by Christian artist Jonathan Pageau reminded me of the words of Ambrose of Milan, 'It is a noble thing to do one's kindnesses and duties toward the whole of the human race. But it is ever more seemly that you should give to God the most precious thing you have, that is, your mind, for you have nothing better than that. When you have paid your debt to your Creator, then you may labour for humanity.' Written in AD 397, these words resonate today. There is a danger that we dethrone God to serve well-intentioned projects helping the needy. Whilst worthy, they remain impoverished gestures without devotion to God our Creator.

We will face confusion as Christians as we come under pressure to serve the needs of the marginalised at the expense of worshipping God, the pinnacle of all that there is and worthy of our praise. It's perhaps easier to do good deeds than worship the unseen Creator, yet without God we have nothing and remain nobody. All meaning is forged within God's heart, and only as we ourselves are washed in the waters of baptism can we become a source of hope to those we seek to serve. There are moments in our lives when we must put God ahead of the moral and ethical demands of Scripture, for in denying God we extinguish the light of God's Word and the biblical ethical framework collapses. This has implications as we engage a secular world with the Jesus gospel.

SCRIPTURE TO CONSIDER: Ps. 63:1–5; Prov. 8:12–36; Luke 9:57–62; John 15:9–19.

AN ACTION TO TAKE: Is prayer as an expression of your worship the priority in your daily life? If not, why is that? Loving God and surrendering entirely is the source of our strength in God.

A PRAYER TO MAKE: 'Lord, may I learn to worship You as my highest good, and the basis from which I can serve the world practically and effectively. Amen.'

John 12:1–6
'"Why wasn't this perfume sold and the money given to the poor? It was worth a year's wages." He did not say this because he cared about the poor but because he was a thief; as keeper of the money bag, he used to help himself to what was put into it.' (vv5–6)

Mary of Bethany approached Jesus and anointed His feet with expensive nard, an aromatic ointment with a musky scent and floral top notes. Washing a guest's feet from the dirt of the dusty streets was a sign of welcome. However, the Torah cautioned against being wasteful, which is what Mary is accused of here. In reality she was symbolically anointing Jesus for His burial. This is the same woman commended by Jesus for taking time to contemplate, whilst her sister Martha, still working hard, was caring for Jesus' practical needs (Luke 10:38–42). Her devotion was welcomed and commended by Jesus on both occasions. Prayerful consideration of Jesus is our primary purpose. Judas, Jesus' betrayer, rebukes Mary with his self-righteous claim that her actions were wasteful and at the cost of the poor. However, Jesus' treasurer was only able to see the perfume's price, not the value of Mary's extravagant act of worship. Judas used the 'poor' for his own convenience. No doubt he distributed some crumbs of comfort to them, yet he was more interested in the quality of life he might create for himself through abusing their vulnerability for his own material benefit. There's always a danger that even the good we propose and intend will in fact only go to serve our own needs. In contemplating Christ, we offer ourselves entirely to God's purpose on earth. Only in contemplating Jesus can we understand the depth of His love and effectively realise our vocation. Good ideas aren't guaranteed to be God's ideas.

SCRIPTURE TO CONSIDER: Lev. 8:1–13; Ps. 133; Matt. 26:6–13; Luke 7:36–50.

AN ACTION TO TAKE: There is always a danger that serving others can be more for our own gratification than for their long-term benefit. This is never God's approach.

A PRAYER TO MAKE: 'Lord, help me to be content to remain anonymous so that might deeds of kindness remain unknown to everyone but you. Amen'

Matthew 6:19–24
**'For where your treasure is, there your heart will be also.
The eye is the lamp of the body. If your eyes are healthy,
your whole body will be full of light.' (vv21–22)**

I n the fifth century AD, Jerome wrote, 'This must be understood not of money only, but of all our possessions. The god of a glutton is his gut; of a lover his lust; and so every man serves that to which he is in bondage; and has his heart there where his treasure is.' Here's our daily challenge: where to place our confidence and our aspiration. In a material age, wealth, both money and accumulated possessions, cause many anxieties. Fear of insufficient financial resources haunts us, even when by comparison with the global majority we are rich beyond comparison; 85% of the world's population lives on less than $30 per day, two-thirds on less than $10 per day, and every tenth person on less than $1.90 per day. For these statistics, price differences between countries are taken into account to adjust for in-country purchasing power.* Learning to locate our treasure in God alone depends on where we choose to gaze. So often distracted by life's perceived instability, our temptation is to take decisions independent of God in our attempt to make adequate provision for ourselves and our families. If the mind is blinded by such worries, the clouds of dark distress rush in and we are consumed in a storm, forever straining to catch sight of Jesus in the encircling gloom. Each day, we require the discipline of deciding if God might be our complete heart's desire, and then ensuring we remain in Christ, come what may (John 15:4).

SCRIPTURE TO CONSIDER: Ps. 27:1–5; Prov. 3:1–30; Matt. 6:25–34; Rev. 2:1–7.

AN ACTION TO TAKE: When you take time to consider surrendering your wellbeing and welfare to God, what questions pop into your head creating anxious thoughts? How do you respond?

A PRAYER TO MAKE: 'Lord, may my every thought and action be taken in the light of Your Word and not in response to my own anxieties. Amen.'

* edwj.org/ja22-9jul [accessed 2022/02/22].

Deception

Judges 18:14–21
'They answered him, "Be quiet! Don't say a word. Come with us, and be our father and priest. Isn't it better that you serve a tribe and clan in Israel as priest rather than just one man's household?" The priest was very pleased. He took the ephod, the household gods and the idol and went along with the people.' (vv19–20)

In life it's easy to be deceived; both by others and, sadly, by ourselves. Micah's Levite priest illustrates this. Having accepted Micah's request to become his priest, the Levite chooses effectively to run a cultic site (Judg. 17:1–10), disobeying God's instructions (Num. 35:5–8). It's worth noting this was at a time when there was no leadership in Israel (Judg. 17:6). We are led through our obedience to the Holy Spirit both in Scripture and the Church's teachings. When we stray from these, however good and godly, there's the opportunity that we will serve our own interests, not God's. Eventually this Levite takes a decision once again in his best interest, accepting an invitation from the Danites to serve them. As they explain, his choice is simple; serve a mere individual or a whole tribe. Self-interest offers apparent advancement, a risk-laden path to tread. Self-interest is our constant companion through life, something we must acknowledge and face, for no-one is incorruptible. However we seek to justify self-interest, it flies in the face of God's best for us. It's why Jesus speaks of our need to die to self if we are to follow Him (Luke 9:23–24). This is everyday martyrdom, the word meaning to witness. Our witness must always be to bring glory to God, although often to do so requires costly, personal sacrifice. It is only in finding God's way that we are led into God's presence. This is the objective of the Christian life.

SCRIPTURE TO CONSIDER: Ps. 43; Jer. 9:1–9; Eph. 5:1–20; Heb. 11:23–40.

AN ACTION TO TAKE: We are easily taken in, and so we need to remain vigilant to resist the temptation to serve self before God. Where are you most challenged by deception?

A PRAYER TO MAKE: 'Lord, I choose to direct my steps in following You and ask that You will guide me every step of the way. Amen.'

Take Care

Joshua 22:3–6
'But be very careful to keep the commandment and the law that Moses the servant of the LORD gave you: to love the LORD your God, to walk in obedience to him, to keep his commands, to hold fast to him and to serve him with all your heart and with all your soul.' (v5)

Taking care demands caution, something I have had to discover for myself. It demands a disciplined approach, to pause long enough to consider all angles. Joshua is an experienced servant of God. Apprenticed to Moses (Num. 11:28) and then selected to lead God's people, he reminds them of his own God-given mandate (Josh. 1:7–9). We may conclude that this is the source of his resilience and perseverance through the challenges encountered during occupying the Promised Land (Gen. 15:17–20). Scripture still presents us the same life-giving insights into how God's servants are to live. We are such by our own free choice, and we do well to observe God's Word as our own mandate in how to live life best.

Whilst God's Word is an ancient text made up of the Jewish Bible (or Old Testament) and the writings following Jesus' ministry (New Testament), it is equally contemporary in its insightfulness and instruction. Indeed, it offers us a clear introduction to the reality of God, even though, apart from what we observe in the earthly life of Jesus, it gives little definition to who God is. He remains a mystery, in whom we place our faith and to whom we owe total allegiance, even though, as we deepen our intimacy with God, we grow increasingly aware of the practical challenges and therefore the changes we must make in our own behaviour. Like all organic relationships, God's Word acts as the yeast that causes our hearts to rise towards God to embrace His purpose entirely.

SCRIPTURE TO CONSIDER: Deut. 6:13–25; Ps. 40:1–8; John 12:20–36; Acts 11:19–30.

AN ACTION TO TAKE: Find ways to read, understand and apply God's Word daily; consider the *Search the Scriptures* course. Visit edwj.org/ja22-8jul

A PRAYER TO MAKE: 'Lord, open my eyes so that I can continuously see wonderful things in Your Word. Amen.'

Joshua 4:19–24
'For the LORD your God dried up the Jordan before you
until you had crossed over. The LORD your God did to the
Jordan what he had done to the Red Sea when he dried
it up before us until we had crossed over.' (v23)

Experience is knowledge gained from repeated trials. In our Christian life, whilst such knowledge doesn't come easily, we can find encouragement when observing God's fingerprints on our life experience. It's easy to lose confidence in God when life is difficult. Indeed, part of maturing as a Christian is accepting that we're not immune to life's slings and arrows simply because of our Christian faith and prayers. Indeed, we live with the mystery of prayer when our requested outcomes fail to materialise. The nature of love is to trust the character and integrity of the object of that love, not simply measure it by external benefits. Love is itself a mystery defying definition, hence why so many ask the question, 'How do I know if I'm in love?'

God told Israel that historical events, things they had heard of but never experienced, were sufficient ground on which to build their lives. The same is true for us as we gaze back upon our crucified Saviour. When life supports appear to crumble, and we don't know where to place our confidence, it is time to remind ourselves of God's demonstrable promises recorded in Scripture. These are carried within the mystery of God's revelation, even as the ground appears to open in readiness to consume us. That mystery is strong enough to absorb our anger, fear and frustration. It is in fact all we have in the face of a troubling and unknowable future.

SCRIPTURE TO CONSIDER: Job 12:1–13; Isa. 64:1–12; Luke 1:57–66; Acts 7:39–56.

AN ACTION TO TAKE: What are the key lessons you have learnt through life experience? How have they shaped your understanding of God, yourself and your life?

A PRAYER TO MAKE: 'Lord, I choose to trust Your promises even when they appear out of reach. Amen.'

Learning

2 Timothy 3:10–17
'But as for you, continue in what you have learned and have become convinced of, because you know those from whom you learned it, and how from infancy you have known the Holy Scriptures, which are able to make you wise for salvation through faith in Christ Jesus.' (vv14–15)

Our sources of learning all shape our understanding and create our bank of knowledge. This then drives the choices we make and the lives we choose to lead, including our view and treatment of others. Adam and Eve revealed that the first sign of human corruption is self-preservation when seeking to hide from God (Gen. 3:8). There is humour here, for how can God's created beings hide from their creator in His creation? Rational logic directs their actions, yet rationality is insufficient to comprehend God. Indeed, many of the questions that trouble us are in search of a rational answer, yet God remains beyond reason, given that reason itself is dependent upon God for its very existence. It takes courage to agree with God that Scripture is indeed His revealed Word for our encouragement and direction. It offers us a mystery in that it can only be understood through the mediation of God's Spirit, who remains an integral member of our Trinitarian God. Much of what we do is born out of obedience alone, and this obedience operates from our own deliberate choices. We are guided by our hearts and not our brains in pursuit of God. Often we discern God within the questions we are presented with, rather than in any specific answer. Such answers tend to end our ongoing conversation with God on the basis that we have closed an issue which was helpfully provoking us towards a deeper exploration of God's revelation. Questions are foundational to our learning.

SCRIPTURE TO CONSIDER: Deut. 18:13–25; Prov. 2:1–11; John 5:31–47; 1 Pet. 3:8–22.

AN ACTION TO TAKE: Does your faith depend on answers to life's many questions? Or are you comfortable trusting God in the many questions you carry?

A PRAYER TO MAKE: 'Lord, thank You that You remain a mystery to me, someone who lies beyond explanation. Amen.'

Romans 12:1–8
'Do not conform to the pattern of this world, but be transformed
by the renewing of your mind. Then you will be able to test and
approve what God's will is – his good, pleasing and perfect will.' (v2)

L eave something organic in the wrong place and it decomposes.
Initially unseen, once rot sets in then items are difficult to restore
to pristine condition. This fully represents the reality of our mortal
life. We engage in a battle between 'deformation' and 'reformation'.
Jesus describes how our eye is drawn instinctively to those things
in the world that carry no intrinsic value (Matt. 6:19–20). Given that
we are naturally drawn towards character deformation (Gen. 3:6),
our deliberate, wilful action is required to direct our steps towards
reformation, and Scripture is full of guidance on how we can do this.
Each of us must 'test and approve what God's will is'. This can never
be either assumed or taken for granted, and its foundations lie within
God's Word.

Our self-evaluation is often on the basis of the value others place
upon us. Or through our success at work, in wealth creation, even
our public generosity. However, the only value that matters is the
inestimable significance placed upon us by God. Is this sufficient to
serve our own need for self-esteem? Naturally we seek to measure
ourselves by objective criteria, something that is easily communicated
and appreciated by others. Yet, since all the good that we do is 'like
filthy rags' before God (Isa. 64:6), we need to learn to find confidence
and satisfaction in God's acceptance and love alone. Humility
expresses itself when we are content to be silent in the face of God's
grace. Being known by God is the summit of meaningful existence.

SCRIPTURE TO CONSIDER: Job 14:13–22; Isa. 64:1–8; 2 Cor. 4:7–18; 1 Pet. 1:13–21.

AN ACTION TO TAKE: If you struggle with insecurity, it is essential to talk this
through with God. What does being loved by the creator of all mean to you
personally?

A PRAYER TO MAKE: 'Lord, may I discover that my real value is only found in
being loved by You. Amen.'

Loving

Romans 12:9–21
**'Never be lacking in zeal, but keep your spiritual
fervour, serving the Lord. Be joyful in hope, patient in
affliction, faithful in prayer. Share with the Lord's people
who are in need. Practise hospitality.' (vv11–13)**

Now accepted by God, Paul provides a list of characteristics that
we can nurture by His grace. Love lies at the centre of God's
activity throughout the world (John 3:16). Once we discover
that we are loved unconditionally, we're invited to respond to that
love through surrendering all of ourselves to God's lordship and
leadership. This is demonstrated in the ways we choose to express
our life, in the attitudes and behaviour they give rise to. So we are to
choose God's way, for every other way is evil. Evil is all that resists God,
and consistently seeks to recapture the heart of Christian disciples.
Sometimes we simply cling to the good, without understanding the
why of our experience. We are equally to love others, expressed in
respect and generosity towards those who suffer.

In a hostile world, Paul invites us to walk in Jesus' footsteps, refusing
to react and respond to evil intention and action directed against us
(Matt. 5:43–48). Indeed, we are to absorb conflict and respond with
lives that model a non-aggressive stance and reveal God's heart and
face of love to a world that runs on angst. Our response may not be
understood, may even be contested forcibly, but we are to persevere
and endure whatever comes our way knowing that God's will ultimately
resolves all struggles and conflicts, if not this side of eternity, most
certainly when the Son of Man returns upon the clouds in glory (Mark
13:24–26).

SCRIPTURE TO CONSIDER: Ps. 34:8–18; Amos 5:13–17; 1 Pet. 4:7–19; 1 John 3:11–24.

AN ACTION TO TAKE: Consider what characteristics your life reveals every day.
Are these the ones God encourages?

A PRAYER TO MAKE: 'Lord, may I learn how love might become my primary reflex
in every circumstance. Amen.'

Joshua 7:10–13
'That is why the Israelites cannot stand against their enemies;
they turn their backs and run because they have been made
liable to destruction. I will not be with you any more unless you
destroy whatever among you is devoted to destruction.' (v12)

There are demands the Christian life places upon us. In seeking
to obey and serve God through our lives we are requested to pay
close attention to every area and note our motivations, attitudes
and activities. Indeed, one reason we may find it a challenge to make
time for God is because we accumulate so many other interests and
so lose sight of Jesus, who is constantly on the move (John 3:8). This
is why we are called to follow Him, which we can only do for as long
as our full attention is directed towards Him. As Israel discovered
on entering the Promised Land, distractions are often the source of
disobedience, and carry consequences. The smallest of idols, no
matter how well hidden, will always undermine our best attempts
faithfully to follow God.

God's response was to invite the Israelites to declutter their lives.
Whenever they searched for surplus idols their resolve and capacity to
live God's way in God's world decreased. There is a principle we can all
relate to; the heavier the load the more tiring our journey. As disciples
we are instructed to adopt the simple way modelled by Jesus. It is
during our ongoing conversation with God that the Spirit can advise us
what is surplus to requirement in actively following Jesus. This is the
decluttering that we ignore to our disadvantage, both in this world and
through eternity. It requires courage, commitment and action. Failure
in this area leads to faith stagnation.

SCRIPTURE TO CONSIDER: Jonah 2; Isa. 45:15–25; Luke 10:1–21; 1 Cor. 10:1–14.

AN ACTION TO TAKE: Give some thought to where the clutter is in your life. Are
there things you need to deal with?

A PRAYER TO MAKE: 'Lord, may I remain vigilant and remove all idols from my life.
Amen.'

Psalm 17:1–5
**'Though you probe my heart, though you examine me
at night and test me, you will find that I have planned
no evil; my mouth has not transgressed.' (v3)**

Our friendship with God is sustained and developed through a continuous conversation (1 Thess. 5:17). Jesus reminds us that it is the 'pure in heart' who 'will see God' (Matt. 5:8). Such purity, a condition where no malice abides and full attention is given to God, is itself a product of our own consideration of how we perceive our relationship with God. David, ruthlessly pursued by Saul and in fear of his life, makes his appeal to God on the basis of his purity of heart. Yet, we know that David later sinned, committing murder and adultery. Such purity of heart is not an accomplishment, a position we attain, but subject to a daily review of our life, primarily in three areas: our attitude, our behaviour, and our words.

This examination best takes place when we are most impressionable, uncertain and, perhaps like David, overwhelmed with challenges whilst lacking any security. Yet, from such formless darkness God created light and shape (Gen. 1:2). The Spirit is present attending to our every heartbeat and the decisions that follow. Such darkness also provides suitable cover for our enemy, Satan, who invites us to assert ourselves in an attempt to take control of our own lives. Such surrender will leave us lost in this darkness of our own choosing. Confronted with his sin, David chose repentance and received forgiveness and restoration. Life is always God's gift, and something we can choose – or reject. Let's acknowledge evil desire and make confession, and choose to be formed in God's image.

SCRIPTURE TO CONSIDER: 2 Sam. 12:1–14; Ps. 51; Luke 6:43–49; 2 Cor. 13:5–10.

AN ACTION TO TAKE: How often are you in conversation with God? We are either moving towards or away from Him.

A PRAYER TO MAKE: 'Lord, I call to You from my darkness and invite Your Spirit to lead me into the light. Amen.'

1 John 4:16–21
'There is no fear in love. But perfect love drives out fear, because fear has to do with punishment. The one who fears is not made perfect in love. We love because he first loved us.' (vv18–19)

Whilst the fear of the Lord is the beginning of wisdom (Prov. 9:10), this isn't fearfulness. It's an awe inspired through our inability to access God combined with His grace in making Himself known. Just as the sun remains inaccessible, we still enjoy the warmth of its rays, and so whilst God lies beyond our comprehension, we feel His presence and marvel at His kindness. Too often we stagnate, uncertain if we are really pursuing God's will. This is not how God wants us to live, for God is love and even as we stray from His path, we discover He comes in search of us, seeking to restore us to His path of righteousness (Luke 15:1–7).

Learning to have complete confidence in God's love is our moment-by-moment challenge. It seems we are far more confident in our own ability to navigate life. It is the waiting that often leads us to make poor decisions, assuming we must do God's work for Him (1 Sam. 13:8–10). Often our anxieties act as the decision takers in our lives, but God says we can confidently trust in Him. To do so demands that we press deeper into appreciating the depth and the substance of God's love for us. It is in our struggles that we are to choose to surrender to God's love. The sun may sink beneath the horizon, or be obscured by clouds, yet it is always there and the warmth of its rays shall return.

SCRIPTURE TO CONSIDER: Exod. 33:7–23; Isa. 45:11–19; Rom. 5:1–11; 1 Tim. 6:6–16.

AN ACTION TO TAKE: What are your greatest challenges when it comes to waiting for God?

A PRAYER TO MAKE: 'Lord, thank You that You are present always and everywhere, and come in search of me when I am lost and confused. Amen.'

My Portion

Joshua 19:49–51
**'When they had finished dividing the land into its
allotted portions, the Israelites gave Joshua son
of Nun an inheritance among them...' (v49)**

We all know the phrase, 'The grass is always greener on the other side of the fence.' The concept is found in the poetry of Ovid (43 BC – 17 AD), who wrote *'Fertilior seges est alenis semper in agris'* ('the harvest is always more fruitful in another man's fields').* Our human heart is always looking for satisfaction beyond the immediacy of our own experience. We may envy another's apparent success or create a 'bucket list' of things we assume will bring us happiness. However, God has ensured that we can find fullness of life within the limits of our own life experience. No longer gazing outwards, scanning the horizon for a satisfying alternative to our lot in life, Scripture tells us that God is found much closer to home. Indeed, He is with us in the everyday realities of our experience. It takes an inner resolve to embrace life as we experience it. Certainly I have struggled with experiences I've weathered, and not always done so with grace or faith to the fore. But, I eventually laid hold of God in my own backyard, even as I looked for more pleasant alternatives elsewhere. This is perhaps one of the most challenging aspects of the Christian life, yet failure to find God where we are will commit us always to be seeking but never finding the fullness Jesus promised (John 10:10). Learning to live confidently in the now is essential, for now is where we are and where we are to find God.

SCRIPTURE TO CONSIDER: Ps. 9:11–20; Jer. 29:1–23; Matt. 7:6–20; 2 Tim. 3.

AN ACTION TO TAKE: Can you find God in your own backyard, or does the grass look greener elsewhere?

A PRAYER TO MAKE: 'Lord, help me to seek You in my own circumstances and so refuse to contrast and compare my situation with those elsewhere. Amen.'

*Ars Amatoria: 1.349–50.

Write to hello@edwj.org and we will write back personally and in confidence as soon as we can.

Ephesians 1:3–10
'For he chose us in him before the creation of the world to be holy and blameless in his sight. In love he predestined us for adoption to sonship through Jesus Christ, in accordance with his pleasure and will...' (vv4–5)

The only way we can rest in God through each season of life is by retaining our confidence in His promise. The fact that we're chosen by God, reveals that we are known; from before time right through to the end of time. This is no random choice, but the expression of an immeasurable love expressed in the person of Jesus; humanity and divinity mystically mixed and expressed in human form. Once found, our decision is simple: will we surrender to God or run from Him? Once we choose God, what will we require to resist the attractions that continuously draw our gaze away from our Saviour?

There's nothing God withholds from His chosen. Yet, we may need to wait patiently on the realisation of God's promise. Indeed, at times His promise is only partially revealed at different times through our lives, and not in the fulness that becomes ours as we cross the threshold from mortality to immortality. Many live clutching a promise, confident only in God's will and ability to fulfil it. There is a mystery here beyond rational understanding, a promise we must cling to even as life pitches us into the sea to wait within the belly of a whale before returning at God's initiative to realise our calling (Jonah 1:17). This is God's way; we stumble only to rise again, just as Jesus humbly descends to earth before rising and returning to God's eternal presence (Phil 2:7–11).

SCRIPTURE TO CONSIDER: Hab. 3; Jonah 2:1–10; Heb. 2:5–18; Jas. 5:7–12.

AN ACTION TO TAKE: When God is silent and appears absent, are you confident in trusting in God's promises?

A PRAYER TO MAKE: 'Lord, though the fig-tree does not bud and there are no grapes on the vines, I will be joyful in God my Saviour. Amen.' (Hab. 3:17–18)

Equipping people to be the positive impact on society through:

- **Nurturing personal growth;**
- **Delivering academic excellence; and**
- **Developing pastoral compassion**

'I was hungry for spiritual growth and to learn – and that expectation has certainly been met.'

Liz, Waverley Abbey College Student

Courses and resources that equip you to be the difference where you are.

waverleyabbeycollege.ac.uk

What our students have done after their training

Mark 8:27–30
'On the way [Jesus] asked them, "Who do people say I
am?" They replied, "Some say John the Baptist; others say
Elijah; and still others, one of the prophets." "But what about
you?" he asked. "Who do you say I am?"' (vv27–29)

One thing is certain: disciples will always carry questions about
their faith. Like children discovering a world with its ever-
expanding horizons, so in our pursuit of God we will need to seek
answers to our many questions. As children besiege their parents with
endless enquiries, so we may cross examine God. All questions are
a provocation for our growth, and if we run out of questions we must
ask if we've lost our way or reduced our faith to a simplistic formula
that simply needs repeating regularly. Every relationship is nurtured
through the questions we ask of the other as well as the questions
that confront us about our own thoughts and actions provoked by the
relationship. Every question fertilises our interest and understanding of
the person, deepening friendship and trust. Our friendship with God is
like this. We have very simple questions at first, and answers are often
supplied by those who encourage us at the start of our faith journey.
As we mature and move through spiritual adolescence towards
adulthood, the depth and importance of our questions intensify. How
might, and why would we frame all of our life around Jesus' simple
invitation, 'Come, follow me' (Matt. 4:19)? We will constantly need to
ask ourselves who Jesus is. Our answer will determine the expression
of our daily discipleship and give shape to how we choose to navigate
life and choose to make our decisions. Over the next few days we'll ask
ourselves some key questions.

SCRIPTURE TO CONSIDER: Ps. 2; Isa. 55:6–13; Luke 9:1–17; John 3:1–20.

AN ACTION TO TAKE: It may be worth keeping a note of your questions and
starting a journal to accompany you on your path of discipleship and keep
track of what God says along the way.

A PRAYER TO MAKE: 'Lord, I have many questions. May I never grow tired of
bringing them to You. Amen.'

Why Learn?

1 Corinthians 10:11–13
'These things happened to them as examples and were written down as warnings for us, on whom the culmination of the ages has come. So, if you think you are standing firm, be careful that you don't fall!' (vv11–12)

Today we're familiar with the term 'lifelong learning'. Formal education may end, but our need to learn continues. Great news for some, for others not so much. Learning serves both personal and professional development. As we live and learn, we grow into and express our full potential. This has two distinct sides to it: choosing to develop into a mature Christian, or electing to increase the distance we place between ourselves and God. Here Scripture warns us that to walk away from God will lead to disappointment, both for us and for God who is calling us. Society seeks to quantify decisions and actions into 'good' or 'bad' as a basis for all morality. Whilst useful as a primer, it can never communicate the impact bad decisions have on us, as well as others. These latter can come to light as the unintended consequences of our decisions and cause further pain. The objective for all learning is not to complete some checkbox exercise demonstrating right from wrong. It is to live with the confidence that our learning will continue through death as we continue to emerge into the fullness for which we were originally created. Learning is always intended for our good and offers the source of our emergence into God's life and purpose. It's easy to believe we have a grasp of our Christian identity and purpose, but this all too easily leads us to take our eyes off Jesus and live by some code of our own manufacture.

SCRIPTURE TO CONSIDER: Ps. 32:3–10; Deut. 8:1–14; Matt. 11:20–30; 1 John 2:20–29.

AN ACTION TO TAKE: How committed are you to lifelong learning? If you need some support visit edwj.org/ja22-19jul, where you can learn to be the difference with God.

A PRAYER TO MAKE: 'Lord, help me to learn from my mistakes and to choose to stay close to You every day. Amen.'

Philippians 2:12–16
'For it is God who works in you to will and to act in order to fulfil his good purpose. Do everything without grumbling or arguing, so that you may become blameless and pure…' (vv13–14)

We follow God to find purpose in life, for faith is all encompassing. Too often we have allowed what is described as the spiritual to be separated from the secular. Yet, secular simply means the culture and society within which we live. There are worshippers of all religions and none, who help shape the world we live within. We are not invited to withdraw and create holy ghettos of our own design in the vain hope that these in some unique way represent God's kingdom on earth. The cross offers the intersection of that which is above and below with that which immediately surrounds us. We are conscious that the perfect kingdom coexists with this fallen world, fallen yet in recovery due to God's redemptive intervention.

Our life, our learning, equips us for service born of love as we discover more of God's relevance within a dissonant world. In Christ we carry a harmonious lyric offering life to us and to our neighbours. God's kingdom impetus is always symbolically to move upwards in pursuit of God's heart and the perfection that frames eternity, whilst at the same time moving outwards into society, beyond our comfort and current understanding, to accomplish the work that God has begun within each one of us. The Spirit works tirelessly to encourage each of us to stay focussed on God's will ahead of any plans of our own, whilst giving birth to actions born of grace that reveal the healing hand of God throughout our cosmopolitan communities.

SCRIPTURE TO CONSIDER: 2 Chron. 30:1–12; Matt. 5:1–16; 1 Cor. 15:42–58; 2 Pet. 1:3–11.

AN ACTION TO TAKE: Interested in expressing God's love through caring by connecting? Look at Paraclesis, an online course, edwj.org/ja22-20jul.

A PRAYER TO MAKE: 'Lord, help me to follow the impulse of Your Spirit in moving upwards towards Your heart, whilst moving outwards to serve Your world. Amen.'

John 13:10–17
'Very truly I tell you, no servant is greater than his master, nor is a messenger greater than the one who sent him. Now that you know these things, you will be blessed if you do them.' (vv16–17)

Learning is far more than an extension of knowledge. The very essence of knowing is application, a demonstration of our learning. How might I take what I know and allow it to influence how I live my life? John Chrysostom, the fourth century bishop of Constantinople, commenting on this passage wrote, 'For to know, belongs to all; but to do, not to all. On this account He said, 'Blessed are you if you do them.' Following Jesus means that what we understand must deeply influence the way we live our lives. This is not simply a moral code we adopt but much more the degree to which we invest our lives into God's purpose. Our understanding of God shapes the outcomes, or causes, in which we invest our time and energy.

Scripture clearly established those characteristics that demonstrate Christian life. Both the Ten Commandments and the Sermon on the Mount provide insight into God's intentions for our welfare, individually and communally. Committing them to memory may act as a useful guide, but they have no substance until we deliberately frame our life actions on them. They are for living, not simply learning. This means seeing beyond the letter of the law to embrace its spirit. The Christian message is fleshed out in our life. Discovering how we might be best enabled to realise God's call through our daily lives is critical to effective discipleship and practical mission. We live to follow Jesus, whilst at the same time being commissioned and sent out by Him.

SCRIPTURE TO CONSIDER: 2 Chron. 31:20–21; Ezra 6:13–22; Gal. 5:13–26; Col. 3:1–17.

AN ACTION TO TAKE: How good are you at putting hands and feet on your learning and living the God-life?

A PRAYER TO MAKE: 'Lord, may I remain focussed upon Your purpose and live to serve it every day. Amen.'

Capability

Romans 12:3–8

'For just as each of us has one body with many members, and these members do not all have the same function, so in Christ we, though many, form one body, and each member belongs to all the others. We have different gifts, according to the grace given to each of us.' (vv4–6a)

Christianity is reflected through the body of Christ, the church. Global in reach, multicultural in substance and denominational in structure, it has the responsibility to make God known. We each enjoy our personal capabilities, which may take time to discover and develop. Each of us also enjoys significance within God's eternal plan. Whilst formed of dust, to which we shall return (Gen. 3:19), we are also invited to rule with Christ (2 Tim. 2:11–13). Remarkably we're engaged in continuous learning or CCD – Continuous Christlike Development! We are invited to learn from God so that we are capable of doing what Jesus invites us to do. We have a record of Jesus' ministry in the Gospel, but He promised that we would do even greater things through our lives (John 14:12). We must never forget that we belong to a Christian community. Often expressed through congregational constructs, we discover that we can do more through co-operation as well as accelerate our learning process in the ways of God. Paolo Freire, an influential philosopher of education, noted that transformational learning happens through 'collaborative, co-produced, inclusive learning communities'. Here, whilst knowledge is shaped by the many, such collaboration must involve conflict, described as 'the midwives of consciousness'.* Many can testify to the conflict within individual congregations, and perhaps more troubling between Christian denominations. It is of course easier to fight amongst ourselves than to join with the Spirit in waging a war with the principalities and powers that rule our world (Eph. 6:12).

SCRIPTURE TO CONSIDER: 1 Sam. 17:32–50; Isa. 5:1–7; 2 Tim. 2:14–26; James 1:19–27.

AN ACTION TO TAKE: God wants to use you in His service personally and through the Church. Are you ready to collaborate with others?

A PRAYER TO MAKE: 'Lord, may I learn to work alongside others in serving You. Amen.' (Phil. 4:9)

* edwj.org/ja22-22jul [accessed 2022/03/26]

Hebrews 1:1–4

'In the past God spoke to our ancestors through the prophets at many times and in various ways, but in these last days he has spoken to us by his Son, whom he appointed heir of all things, and through whom also he made the universe.' (vv1–2)

Surf the net, scan YouTube and search valuable apps and you'll be swamped with ideas, many in the early stages of development. Myriad podcasts also provoke us to consider everything, from our historical roots to our psychological health. We're awash with ideas and propositions seeking to provide a meaning for our lives. This is a question humanity has faced since the dawn of time, the moment self-awareness was born through an act of self-determination (Gen. 3:7). Subsequent to our expulsion from Eden, God has attempted to communicate the meaning He gives to every life, uniquely created in His image. However, the words were only ever believed in part and for short seasons. Ultimately God chose to embody His message of ultimate meaning in the incarnate Jesus, God and man inextricably contained within a mortal life (Luke 1:30–31).

Truth finds full expression through embodiment. Jesus is 'the image of the invisible God' (Col. 1:15), and post Pentecost we are invited to embody the life of God as signposts and witnesses to life's ultimate expression of meaning and purpose. As 'temples of the Holy Spirit' (1 Cor. 6:19), the life of God emanates from within us. Simply put, we are the hands and feet of Jesus, witnesses to Christian hope throughout a troubled, and troubling, world. Therefore, we become sacred through encounter with God, and witness to Him through the life we lead. A source of wonder to both heaven and earth (Ps. 8:5).

SCRIPTURE TO CONSIDER: Ps. 8; Mic. 3:5–8; Acts 2:1–24, 6:14–17; Rev. 21:1–8.

AN ACTION TO TAKE: What does it mean to know that you are the embodiment of God's Spirit on earth? How does this influence your life choices?

A PRAYER TO MAKE: 'Lord, may I be continually filled with Your Spirit, always giving thanks to God the Father for everything. Amen.' (Eph. 5:18–20)

Colossians 2:6–10
'For in Christ all the fullness of the Deity lives in bodily form, and in Christ you have been brought to fullness. He is the head over every power and authority.' (vv9–10)

R ealisation means to exhibit the actual existence of something. In our case it is to exhibit the reality of God in a world of competing ideas, all seeking to lay claim to the meaning of life. In this multiplicity of meanings, we are consistently subject to becoming first captivated and finally captured by 'hollow and deceptive philosophy, which depends on human tradition and the elemental spiritual forces of this world rather than on Christ' (v8b). Yet, in the One who fleshed out God's character on earth for mortal understanding, we have a clear pattern which we are invited to follow. It may initially appear uncomfortable, for it resists the lure of self-gratification in responding to God's appeal that we live to serve God and others. Where Adam blamed God and another in his futile attempt at self-defence (Gen. 3:12), Jesus on the cross surrenders to God, and forgives His executioners, amongst whom we must count ourselves (Luke 23:34), whilst also commending His mother to John's care (John 19:26–27). The cross reaches vertically and horizontally, as must we.

A measure of the fullness of our faith is the degree to which we are able to realise God's presence and purpose within the circumstances we find ourselves in. It is self-evident that we draw nearer to God daily through our obedience. Discipleship is a full-time occupation, carried out within the regular tasks of daily life, family, work and leisure. Living our lives in Christ establishes God's kingdom on earth (Matt. 6:10).

SCRIPTURE TO CONSIDER: S. of S. 2:3–15; Deut. 6:10–25; Eph. 5:6–20; 1 Tim. 6:11–21.

AN ACTION TO TAKE: Review the last few months and consider what has been realised through your life. What have you exhibited?

A PRAYER TO MAKE: 'Lord, may I live in freedom as I seek to exhibit God's reality in my everyday context. Amen.'

Philippians 3:12–14
'Not that I have already obtained all this, or have already
arrived at my goal, but I press on to take hold of that for which
Christ Jesus took hold of me. Brothers and sisters, I do not
consider myself yet to have taken hold of it.' (vv12–13a)

Assessing where we are in our discipleship, we may identify a gap
between where we are and where we want to be. No worries –
Paul felt the same. A Christian hero, he knew that he was in a
marathon, not a sprint, and was invited to keep going till called home by
God. Only those who cross the finish line can claim to have completed
the race. Whilst competing we're cheered on by a great cloud of
witnesses, those faithful servants who preceded us (Heb. 12:1). Feeling
despondent? Remember you are never alone.

Sometimes it's simple to address these gaps. Sometimes we need
advice and then to set aside time and money to train and build our
skillset. Waverley Abbey College (WAC) solely exists for this purpose,
providing simple steps to deepen understanding and practical skills
training, enabling disciples to become more effective in Christian
service. Its purpose is to support the Church in being equipped to fulfil
God's mission call throughout the communities it serves. Working with
pastors and mission leaders, WAC works tirelessly to equip everyday
disciples to serve the world Jesus loves so much (John 3:16). We are
training 1,000 chaplains over the next five years who'll provide a
listening ear and caring heart for people at work, school or in prison,
ready to bear the load that the cares of the world create (Matt. 11:28).
We would love to train you to be Jesus' hands and feet in the world
every day.

SCRIPTURE TO CONSIDER: Acts 7:20–38; Gal. 6:1–10; 1 Tim. 4:1–10; Heb. 5:11–6:8.

AN ACTION TO TAKE: Look at the skills opportunities provided by WAC. Visit edwj.
org/ja22-25jul

A PRAYER TO MAKE: 'Lord, ours the eyes through which You look with
compassion on this world, ours Your hands and feet. Equip and send us
where we can serve You best. Amen.'

Luke 12:32–34
'For where your treasure is, there your heart will be also.' (v34)

A priority is a value we give to something; another word might be 'treasure'. Life demands that we make decisions and choose what we prioritise. A favourite group icebreaker is to ask people that if their house was consumed in flames, what treasured item would they grab before running from the building? Answers offer a glimpse into our priorities. As a Christian we're always challenged over what takes precedence in our lives. Daily we make choices, but the number of offerings is usually large. Here we truly face up to the enemy's attempts to force our hand and act in ways that reduce God's influence over our life, and in the world. Whilst there's always a logical rationale for the decisions we take, we are skilled at whitewashing our actions with carefully crafted words. Christian life is simple in essence. We obey God, our guide being His Word and personal encounter, often determined via our conscience. Informed by cultural norms, this regulates human behaviour. Such norms prove hard to recognise, articulate, and then resist, because they normalise all social understanding and interaction. Conscience builds its knowledge base by observation, and exercises a powerful influence over how we choose, more often subconsciously than consciously. To obey God, we must develop our intuitive response to God's indwelling Spirit, who will never contradict God's eternal Word found in Scripture. Our daily challenge is learning to differentiate between building on experience drawn from observation and instruction of accepted social patterns of behaviour and discerning God's will for us.

SCRIPTURE TO CONSIDER: Prov. 18:1–15; Isa. 30:18–26; John 5:16–30; Heb. 4:14–16.

AN ACTION TO TAKE: In discerning God's ways within the social and cultural context in which we live, what do we accommodate, where do we assimilate and when do we resist?

A PRAYER TO MAKE: 'Lord, teach me how to listen to You in the hustle and bustle of everyday life, and to prioritise my spiritual aspirations and learning. Amen.'

Write to hello@edwj.org and we will write back personally and in confidence as soon as we can.

Acts 2:42–47
'They devoted themselves to the apostles' teaching and to fellowship, to the breaking of bread and to prayer. Everyone was filled with awe at the many wonders and signs performed by the apostles. All the believers were together and had everything in common.' (vv42–44)

The early disciples were of one mind, or 'together' (v44). The word is found in Acts 1:14, again in Acts 4:32 and many other instances and it means 'of one passion'. Together they shared a common interest in following Jesus. Yet, the Gospel stories reveal that, whilst the twelve disciples were together in following Jesus, they were of different temperaments. Sharing a passion will look different in every individual case. How we learn to follow Jesus will vary from one disciple to the next. In any garden, plants require different soil and weather conditions to flourish. We're similar! This is one reason why we find certain ways of learning more helpful than others. I'm primarily kinaesthetic, and so learn by doing. Sitting in classrooms frustrates me, as does teaching others. It's one reason I lived in community for twenty-five years – learning Christian life alongside others. Whilst sharing common values we must ensure we find a style of learning that suits us, and today there are so many options: digital, roll-on-roll-off courses, distance learning with webinars, or the more traditional classroom approach. The only essential is that I walk away better skilled in applying my knowledge to express my gifts in service of God. Increasingly the structured academic world of Higher Education is recognising that for many employers it's not the letters after a name that count, but the ability to apply knowledge in practice. This is always the best measure of effective learning.

SCRIPTURE TO CONSIDER: Luke 2:41–52; 1 Cor. 4:14–21; 1 Tim. 4:11–16; 2 Tim. 2:14–26.

AN ACTION TO TAKE: One book I value is Dietrich Bonhoeffer's *Life Together*. If you are looking for knowledge of God rooted in knowledge of the self, read it. edwj.org/ja22-27jul

A PRAYER TO MAKE: 'Lord, help me to understand how I learn best and then seek to grow in my understanding by using this style. Amen.'

1 Corinthians 10:31–11:2

'For I am not seeking my own good but the good of many, so that they may be saved. Follow my example, as I follow the example of Christ. I praise you for remembering me in everything and for holding to the traditions just as I passed them on to you.' (vv10:33b–11:2)

Examples offer help in illustrating what's being said. They assist us in how to practise our learning. Paul confidently invited the Corinthians to follow his example, as he followed Jesus' example. Jesus is the only visual aid we have for the characteristic behaviour expected of disciples. We often believe the bar is set too high, aimed at 'super-saints', and not the average mortal. Yet, this is the life that every Christian disciple is expected to embrace, albeit through an ongoing change process affecting thought and action. When we assume that the life described in Scripture is beyond our reach, we identify our lack of confidence in God's ability to change us from the inside out.

Paul, through his life and letters, attempts to describe discipleship for all the Christian community. Times change, but not God's message. Why does it take us so long to take our words of adoration and commitment and implement them as our daily devotion and service? Today I'm creaking beneath the accumulated rings of age, yet only over the last fifteen years have I been sufficiently enamoured and captivated with an inner desire to live entirely for God. I cannot comment on my success, an account will be available at my death and without reference to my own rose-tinted memoirs. I now believe with a depth of conviction and an intensity unknown in my earlier life. This realisation helps me to take appropriate steps to roll out my planned discipleship in obedience to God.

SCRIPTURE TO CONSIDER: Deut. 27:9–28:14; 1 Kgs 8:54–61; Matt. 15:1–20; Rom. 14:5–23.

AN ACTION TO TAKE: What are the next steps you want to roll out in your discipleship plan?

A PRAYER TO MAKE: 'Lord, deepen my love for You as daily I choose to live for You. Amen.'

Psalm 119:57–64
'I have sought your face with all my heart; be gracious to
me according to your promise. I have considered my ways
and have turned my steps to your statutes. I will hasten
and not delay to obey your commands.' (vv58–60)

How do we evaluate, or find a value for, our learning and
subsequent service? Effective measures are hard to find for
something not calculated against external criteria. Only God
knows the state of our heart and can compute our integrity. Jesus
tells us to keep quiet about the apparent good we do so that we don't
congratulate ourselves or allow pride to provoke us into judging
others. We can easily evaluate where and when we miss the mark by
observing how frequently we criticise or envy others, and then talk
about our own accomplishments. We exist to serve God and to Him
alone we will account for our life. One useful measure is the degree to
which I'm confident and comfortable in remaining anonymous, known
only to God.

   This negative approach perhaps best guides us in measuring
our faithfulness in serving God. The things I'm most aware of once
enlivened to God's way are the ones I know act as barriers between us.
It's a matter of personal choice if I want to demolish such barriers, for
in doing so I must sacrifice elements in life that purely nourish my ego.
Early in the gospel story John the Baptist gives us the best benchmark
to evaluate our Christian growth and effectiveness (John 3:30); it is the
degree to which I am decreasing, becoming anonymous, for as I move
from my life's centre stage, I ensure I leave room for only one, Jesus,
and He alone is floodlit by the super trouper.

SCRIPTURE TO CONSIDER: Ps. 49:1–12; Prov. 21:1–16; Matt. 15:1–20; 2 Cor. 13:1–10.

AN ACTION TO TAKE: It takes courage to decrease, especially when so many are
intent on increasing their visibility. Are you hungry to decrease or increase?

A PRAYER TO MAKE: 'Lord, may I learn to be content that my influence is greatest
when I quietly and obediently step aside for You in my life. Amen.'

John 10:10-18

'I am the good shepherd. The good shepherd lays down his life for the sheep. The hired hand is not the shepherd and does not own the sheep. So when he sees the wolf coming, he abandons the sheep and runs away. Then the wolf attacks the flock and scatters it.' (vv11-12)

When exploring any educational or training programme we always make a cost-benefit analysis. Is the investment of time, finance, and energy worth the return? We quantify this across a spectrum ranging from practical outcomes to personal achievement. I went back to university part time as a necessary distraction from the intensity of caring for my wife. Whilst the content engaged me because I love study for its own sake, time spent with people who knew nothing of my situation was a refreshing break from the incessant enquiries from well-meaning friends. The surprising outcome was that God introduced me to the Eastern Orthodox Church and a way of thinking theologically which deeply ministered to me in a difficult season. I found my path at the point of my deepest need.

Attempting to learn more about the God we serve and how we might become more like Him, daily presents us with personal challenges. The intention to know God better will have unexpected and unintended consequences. We will find things about ourselves that might shock as much as satisfy. We'll be shown a path we never knew existed, an access point into the hidden wonders of Narnia. Here we'll be equipped even as we are tested in the realm of our understanding and chosen way of life. Seldom will we emerge as we anticipated at the start of our learning journey, but without it we are likely to grow stale, even stagnant, and our faith will most likely wither away (1 John 2:19).

SCRIPTURE TO CONSIDER: Isa. 46:5-13; Hab. 2:2-5; John 11:17-44; Gal. 2:11-21.

AN ACTION TO TAKE: There are intangible, as well as tangible, consequences to pursuing God. Are you willing to enter into the discomfort that accompanies all learning?

A PRAYER TO MAKE: 'Lord, I choose to move from my comfort zone in search of a fuller understanding of myself and of You. Amen.'

E-Learning Short Courses

Feed your mind in your own time and at a pace that suits you best. Ideal for individuals, small groups and congregations.

 **Insight Courses**

 **Paraclesis: A series on pastoral care**

 **The Prayers of Jesus**

 **Eat, Pray, Share**

These and other courses are all available for you online at a price of £25 each.

To find out more and to buy a course, visit

wvly.org/online-courses

Ecclesiastes 12:9–14
**'The words of the wise are like goads, their collected sayings
like firmly embedded nails – given by one shepherd. Be
warned, my son, of anything in addition to them.' (vv11–12)**

F riendship with Jesus provokes us into building credible lives
of service reflecting His character. All four Gospel accounts
present a picture of how Jesus lived, yet we quickly discover we
lack the power to live His way without the power of the Holy Spirit,
deposited within us by God's grace when we say yes to Him (Rom.
8:9). Of course, we start as newborns in the Christian life (John 3:3)
and are encouraged to grow through childhood and adolescence
into adulthood (1 Cor. 3:1–3). Physically we may have the attributes of
an adult but behave like an ill-tempered toddler. Learning to live the
Christian life is discerning and serving Jesus consistently.

Despite knowing how to behave, we will also encounter times that
test us to our limit. We might hope for 'normal circumstances', but
there's no such thing. We are all inclined towards conservatism deep
within our human make up, a desire to protect ourselves from things
that appear to destabilise and threaten our existence, from sickness to
financial instability. If such conditions consume us, it becomes more
difficult to apply our Christian learning and understanding. We can feel
isolated, with few sources of encouragement to calm our legitimate
fears and keep hope alive. Each of us will need to learn to practise our
faith in both calm and storm conditions. Context will impact and shape
our faith with Jesus, always providing our example whilst also guiding
us (John 16:33).

SCRIPTURE TO CONSIDER: Job 40:1–5, 42:1–6; 1 Cor. 13:4–13; Eph. 4:14–32.

AN ACTION TO TAKE: Kickstart your spiritual growth with *Strengthen Your Core*
by Jenny Campbell edwj.org/ja22-31jul

A PRAYER TO MAKE: 'Lord, lead me into maturity in every circumstance. Amen.'

Write to hello@edwj.org and we will write back personally and in confidence as soon as we can.

1 Corinthians 14:18–21
**'Brothers and sisters, stop thinking like children. In regard
to evil be infants, but in your thinking be adults.' (v20)**

Today we're inundated with valuable resources online, in print, and at conferences. There's almost too much information and a danger we may try to live a life that is not our own. Consider David, trained as a shepherd to protect sheep from wild animals, then dressed in Saul's armour which severely restricted his movement and compromised his skills (1 Sam. 17:38–40). God asks us to reflect on our learning and weave the lessons learnt into our daily practice. Each of us is unique and will discover an individual pattern for obediently serving Jesus. Protecting sheep might not have seemed the ideal preparation for confronting giants, yet it was precisely this that gave David his victory.

Growth in God is different in every case; what inspires one will tire another. We are to treat each other with respect and never propose a singular way of service. We don't know how God is preparing His disciples for their work (Eph. 2:10). So, God invites and expects us to listen and learn, both by doing and learning, so that we may determine how best to live the Christian life every day. I found myself drawn into resolving disagreements, and, feeling unprepared, I searched for help and found mediation. Having trained I worked for eighteen years in conflict resolution. This followed a season as an evangelist and church leader. So, God equips us, yet we must determine what God wants with us and where we can find support in developing our skill sets.

SCRIPTURE TO CONSIDER: Exod. 3:1–15; 1 Sam. 17:12–51; 2 Thess. 1:11–12; Heb. 6:1–12.

AN ACTION TO TAKE: It can fell daunting to take responsibility for our own spiritual development, but this is a sign of Christian maturity.

A PRAYER TO MAKE: 'Lord, I will make every effort to confirm Your calling in my life. Help me if I stumble, and daily strengthen my confidence in You. Amen.' (2 Pet. 1:10)

Timekeeping

Joshua 4:19–24
'For the LORD your God dried up the Jordan before you until you had crossed over. The LORD your God did to the Jordan what he had done to the Red Sea when he dried it up before us until we had crossed over.' (v23)

A friend once said to me, 'God's clock keeps perfect time', referring to how we often need to wait for God to act. Our temptation is to step in when God appears slow in showing up. Joshua and the Israelites have now safely crossed the Jordan and, like their earlier Red Sea crossing, witnessed a miracle. Miracles are encouraging momentarily but Israel spent forty years wandering in the wilderness in between, and only Joshua and Caleb had experienced God's first miracle. Our impatience can hijack God's purpose, an impatience that expresses intolerance at having to wait.

Confidence in God requires owning our impatience, especially when our lives appear to be at risk by waiting. Much prayer is born of urgency in an attempt to twist God's arm. However, the bedrock of all prayer is a willingness to trust God, even when silent, aka the 'sleep in death' (Ps. 13:3b). Here our life is suspended by a thread as we wait for God. In such times our confidence must be uncomfortably placed in God's reputation, like Joshua's standing stones. The testimony of those who have trusted God over time offers us one source of comfort in the instability of our own waiting game. God is true to Himself and when waiting gives rise to disappointment can we trust God in our despondency? There is hope born in the witness of the lives of others who find faith, no bigger than a mustard seed, whilst experiencing the mystery of failed expectation.

SCRIPTURE TO CONSIDER: Ps. 13; Jer. 17:5–8; 2 Cor. 12:1–10; 1 Pet. 5:6–11.

AN ACTION TO TAKE: How does it feel to know you are not the master of your own destiny but dependent upon God in all things?

A PRAYER TO MAKE: 'Lord, look on me and answer; give light to my eyes, or I will sleep in death. Amen.' (Ps. 13:3)

Psalm 46:1–11
**'God is our refuge and strength, an ever-present help in
trouble. Therefore we will not fear, though the earth give way
and the mountains fall into the heart of the sea…' (vv1–2)**

A refuge is a place we run back to. As an injured child turns to a
parent for comfort, so we, confused by an unresolved mystery,
can run back to God, who offers reassurance and comfort, though
the source of our pain remains unresolved. We need to find some
comfort when our reaction to such pain is an outburst of emotion. Our
immediate response may be to flee from God to punish Him in some
way, or to fall into His arms sobbing with the unresolved confusion that
consumes our whole body, mind and spirit. By the nineteenth century a
refuge meant a temporary shelter for the destitute or homeless, an apt
description of our situation when our life implodes. But it is temporary
because the expectation is that once the storm's fury has passed, we'll
recover our composure and find a narrative that enables us to continue
on our way.

Trouble is all consuming, demanding everything from us. We've
little time to pause and think, because we must navigate a crisis,
external and internal, and we are shocked by the demands it makes
on our human resources. But God remains 'an ever-present help in
trouble'. We may need to struggle to discern Him at the height of
personal storms – one reason we take time daily in deepening our
communication and friendship so that in moments of crisis, turning to
God is our instinctive reflex, as unconscious, yet certain, as fleeing a
burning building; an instinctive act of self-preservation.

SCRIPTURE TO CONSIDER: Ps. 18:1–19; Ps. 119:25–32; John 14:5–14; Phil. 4:4–13.

AN ACTION TO TAKE: What is your instinctive reaction when the storms of life
engulf you? Consider how you will make God your first port of call in future
trouble.

A PRAYER TO MAKE: 'Lord, my soul is weary with sorrow; strengthen me
according to Your word. Amen.' (Ps. 119:28)

Psalm 14:1–4
'The LORD looks down from heaven on all mankind to see
if there are any who understand, any who seek God. All
have turned away, all have become corrupt; there is
no one who does good, not even one.' (vv2–3)

Making sense of life presents a challenge for us all, one that stretches well beyond our years of anticipated adolescent struggles with meaning and identity. Whilst we seek to manage our life and keep it within the safety of the banks between which it flows, sudden storms can cause a flood and the river is replaced by a borderless lake that drowns everything beneath its waters. When faced with flood we seek to preserve our life and it raises questions around the source of our security. Every crisis poses the same question: where can I find the safety I crave? Perhaps there is no chance that my preferences can be realised. Therefore, I am left to cling to God, my lifebelt in uncharted waters, or to strike out on my own in the hope of making land before I tire and drown.

It's humbling to acknowledge that I must seek God, even in those times when I don't know for certain that I understand Him or His ways. Learning to cling to a promise in unsettling seasons is part of our discipleship. How else will God test the seriousness of my profession of faith? It takes time to discover if I actually have the confidence to live by God's promise alone. In doing so I must travel by way of dispossession, where I'm stripped of everything superfluous to faith in Christ alone (John 20:31). Can my security be firmly located in Christ?

SCRIPTURE TO CONSIDER: Exod. 15:1–18; Prov. 11:1–11; Eph. 2:1–10; Jas 4:13–17.

AN ACTION TO TAKE: Where is your security located? What are the struggles you have as you travel the path of dispossession so that you can fully take hold of Jesus?

A PRAYER TO MAKE: 'Lord, You are worthy to receive glory and honour and power, for You created all things, and by Your will they were created and have their being. Amen.' (Rev. 4:11)

Genesis 2:15–18
'And the LORD God commanded the man, "You are free to eat from any tree in the garden; but you must not eat from the tree of the knowledge of good and evil, for when you eat from it you will certainly die."' (vv16–17)

We've observed that God places decision taking squarely in our hands. This free will precedes the Fall, demonstrating God has no interest in micro-managing His creation. In his state of innocence, Adam heard God's advice with nothing to compare it to or contradict it. He was comfortable taking God at His word, yet trouble loomed. Obedience operates as an expression of a love that is never enforced, always a free, individual choice. I was living in community when Katey, my first wife, physically deteriorated with MS, and community members took the decision to stay and help us, despite my encouraging them to leave and get on with their lives. Coercion only produces servitude, which in turn generates resentment and the imbalance of injustice. In turn this leads to impaired decision making, for the injury such injustice causes affects good judgment. In rare cases it produces witness to the purity of justice itself, for example Nelson Mandela, who resisted his claim for justifiable retribution.

God does not take retribution on us because of our free will choices. Nor are we, the Church, to judge others. We're to encourage everyone with Christ's claims and the Christian approach to life, but we are never to coerce anyone to believe or punish someone for the choices they make. Naturally society has its own processes for prosecuting criminals, but even here Jesus demonstrates mercy in response to repentance and faith with no evidence of reformation of a criminal's life (Luke 23:42–43).

SCRIPTURE TO CONSIDER: Josh. 24:14–22; Prov. 16:9–25; Gal. 5:13–26; 2 Peter 3:3–14.

AN ACTION TO TAKE: On what basis do you make decisions? Where is God in the process?

A PRAYER TO MAKE: 'Lord, thank You for the room to make decisions. Guide me to the best ones so that my steps might be established. Amen.' (Prov. 16:9)

First and Last

1 Corinthians 15:45–49
'The spiritual did not come first, but the natural, and after that the spiritual. The first man was of the dust of the earth; the second man is of heaven.'(vv46–47)

In learning how to live the Christian life we're given two examples – Adam and Jesus, the first and the last Adam. Whilst the first introduced death and decay into humanity, the second illustrated the possibility of heaven on earth. There is a way of living that reflects God's character on earth, but this turns on our personal decisions. Augustine of Hippo (AD 354–430) wrote, 'First comes the clay that is only fit to be thrown away, with which we must begin but in which we need not remain. Afterward comes what is fit for us, that into which we can be gradually moulded and in which, when moulded, we may remain'.* Change is a process, one that requires our personal leadership. It is not simply a decision to follow Jesus, but an ongoing series of decisions that determine our standing in God.

Being moulded is an excellent analogy for the Christian life. God is the master potter and we're the clay on His wheel, always subject to regular reshaping until ready to be fired and fulfil our shape's purpose, just as a jug carries fluid and a plate holds food. The exciting thing is that none of us knows what shape God has in mind for our life. Only by yielding to the hands of the master potter can we be assured of being moulded into that shape and fulfilling our purpose on earth. Even more encouraging is that our mortality shows our humanity, whilst our obedience reveals the divine source of our life.

SCRIPTURE TO CONSIDER: Isa. 29:13–16; Jer. 18:1–10; Rom. 6:1–14; 2 Cor. 5:16–21.

AN ACTION TO TAKE: Who is God shaping you into? And for what purpose? Agree to allow the master potter to shape and equip you for His service.

A PRAYER TO MAKE: 'Lord, help me to walk in freedom, for I delight in Your commands because I love them. Amen.' (Psa. 119:45–48)

* *City of God*, 15.1.

Genesis 3:1–6
'When the woman saw that the fruit of the tree was good for food and pleasing to the eye, and also desirable for gaining wisdom, she took some and ate it. She also gave some to her husband, who was with her, and he ate it.'(v6)

Self-determination is critical to psychological wellbeing and personal growth.* Human development requires that we must feel in control of our behaviour, free will. Eve takes control of her environment and approves the fruit which she takes and eats, taking direct action for herself. This process teaches us how to master tasks and exercise our independence from others. So a child grows in confidence and learns skills necessary to leave home and live independently. In achieving her goal, tasting the fruit that looked good to eat, Eve learned and demonstrated confidence and independence. However, whilst action may be independently initiated, we always want to experience participation with others, a sense of community, and so Adam joins her in the experience and they enjoy a sense of belonging together through shared experience. The unrecognised problem for Eve and Adam is that they breach a foundational instruction given by God; foundational since it is part of the Creator's instructions. In exercising free will we must still work within certain parameters established to enable us to realise our fullest potential. Only God knows what our potential is, and it can only be realised by applying the lessons for growth set out by God in Scripture. In this instance we know that whilst the process of self-determination is necessary, it was exercised in disobedience to God's instructions and therefore triggered consequences that lay beyond Eve's understanding. We learn that self-determination carries an intrinsic responsibility within it, whose consequences can be both good and bad.

SCRIPTURE TO CONSIDER: 1 Sam. 10:8–27, 13:4–15; Acts 5:1–11; Luke 6:46–49.

AN ACTION TO TAKE: Self-determination is essential for growth, but we will not grow if we step outside of God's principles that alone ensure fullness of life (John 10:10).

A PRAYER TO MAKE: 'Lord, I want to keep Your commandments. May I walk closely with the Holy Spirit, and be led into all Your truth. Amen.' (John 14:15–17)

* Edward L. Deci & Richard M. Ryan, *Intrinsic Motivation and Self-Determination in Human Behaviour* (Springer, 1985).

Sin and Righteousness

Romans 6:15–20
'Don't you know that when you offer yourselves to someone as obedient slaves, you are slaves of the one you obey – whether you are slaves to sin, which leads to death, or to obedience, which leads to righteousness?' (v16)

Self-determination poses the question of just how independent we are. We can't make a decision to break the law without facing consequences, the price of policing in a social contract we support with its promise of peace, prosperity, and privacy. However, there are internal and external factors at play seeking to influence our 'independent' decisions. In Eden it was the external voice of Satan, with us it can be internal appetites and external influencers. All decisions are the result of a response to stimuli, and once taken they're subject to review and reframe. Once implemented our decisions impact us and others. They form a shape which influences the world in which we live.

Paul states that we're never autonomous because all our decisions are subject to influencers. Today our social media pandemic overstimulates us with information, its validity impossible to establish. Media moves at an astonishing speed in pursuit of our need to know now. Like chicks, our beaks are open, constantly craving to be fed! We often seek relevance not reality. In Christ we discover the bedrock for all truth, or reality Himself. Only by learning to respond to the stimulus of the Holy Spirit will we find a trustworthy source to operate our freedom to self-determination effectively. There are overarching frameworks that promise a heaven on earth, from communism to capitalism, however neither has afforded the complete personal freedom that comes through serving the Lord of righteousness, and it is His pattern for life we are to follow.

SCRIPTURE TO CONSIDER: 2 Chr. 20:15–21; Isa. 41:8–10; Luke 21:5–33; Rom 12:9–21.

AN ACTION TO TAKE: The hard work begins with our attempt to isolate and identify the influencers, internal and external, that drive our life decisions. Are you up for the challenge?

A PRAYER TO MAKE: 'Lord, I want to hold to Your teaching as a disciple so that I may know the truth, and the truth will set me free. Amen.' (John 8:31–32)

Freedom

2 Corinthians 3:12–18
**'Now the Lord is the Spirit, and where the Spirit of the
Lord is, there is freedom. And we all, who with unveiled
faces contemplate the Lord's glory, are being transformed
into his image with ever-increasing glory, which comes
from the Lord, who is the Spirit.' (vv17–18)**

Hope is our greatest imagined good, the source for our optimism.
Pandemics, wars, and life's many challenges quickly dampen
such optimism. However, hope is something that can help keep us
focussed on the good we visualise. It's never a choice between hope
or despair, although when tragedy strikes, despondency sweeps in
like a flood and we must acknowledge it. If we are to grow in God we
must learn to withstand the flood tide of despair, knowing that there is
still a life that we will live, albeit we may have to overwrite our previous
narrative to move on. This requires resilience, the discovery that we can
continue to grow in the face of adversity.

When Scripture speaks of the veil that covered Moses face, it refers
to the Law, for until Jesus' ministry no one could gaze on God and live
(Exod. 33:20). We now enjoy access to God directly, and can learn
through the Spirit how to live in each chapter of our lives. The hope
we carry is not some self-induced idealised dream, but the fact that
our lives are now hidden with Christ in God (Col. 3:3), whilst daily being
transformed into Christlikeness as we abide in God (John 15:5). Once
we know that our lives are secured through God's grace and our future
guaranteed, then we seize our freedom in life, for whatever is directed
against us, whilst real and painful in experience, doesn't ever have the
power to remove us from God's loving acceptance.

SCRIPTURE TO CONSIDER: Exod. 34:29–35; Ps. 27:1–14; Eph. 1:3–14; Heb. 13:1–16.

AN ACTION TO TAKE: What challenges the hope you carry in your heart? Do you
enjoy freedom in your life? If not, what are the reasons?

A PRAYER TO MAKE: 'Lord, You created me for freedom. Help me to refuse the
yoke of slavery and write a God-centered narrative for my life. Amen.'

Genesis 3:7–10
**'Then the eyes of both of them were opened, and they
realised that they were naked; so they sewed fig leaves
together and made coverings for themselves.' (v7)**

Having eaten from the forbidden tree of the knowledge of good
and evil, their eyes are opened and they see their nakedness, a
vulnerability of which they'd been unconscious in their former
state of innocence. Always seeing what was around them, now they
had sight of their inner makeup, conscious of wrong and right. Things
once seen can never be unseen. As humans we learn that if we pursue
unhelpful, often unhealthy, experiences, then we cannot erase their
memory and their effects on us are long lasting. For some this is the
source of their addiction, for others the start of living a life of regret.
Consciously naked, they felt the first shame (v10) and had the first
encounter with guilt.

Guilt drives us towards confession or deceit. Now 'afraid',
a consequence of sin, they attempt to deceive God by hiding, for they
cannot ignore God's voice. God's beautiful mission is to send Jesus
who sets us free from shame and guilt, inviting us into a friendship that
rescues us from our nakedness and provides deliverance from all our
fears. We must daily ask ourselves, surrounded by temptation, how is
it we want to live? Decision made, our schooling in discipleship begins.
Jesus lived as human and divine, demonstrating how we might live in
obedience to God. Disobedience will always open the door beyond
which our self-destruction is guaranteed. God promises to encourage
us wherever and whenever we choose obedience, though the price for
our return to Paradise will prove costly.

SCRIPTURE TO CONSIDER: Deut. 30:11–20; Isa. 30:19–26; Rom. 5:12–21; Gal. 6:1–10.

AN ACTION TO TAKE: Far from God and ashamed of your nakedness? Choose to
return to God and benefit from His fully comprehensive rescue plan.

A PRAYER TO MAKE: 'Lord, may I daily choose to enter by the narrow gate and
avoid the wide gate that so easily leads to my destruction. Amen.' (Matt. 7:13)

Lost Innocence

Genesis 3:21–24
**'The Lord God made garments of skin for Adam
and his wife and clothed them.' (v21)**

On discovering their nakedness, Adam and Eve immediately attempted to cover a shame they'd never known. Knowledge of good can only exist with a knowledge of its counterpart, evil. They fashioned fig leaves into clothing, a sign of lost innocence. Figs symbolise life, prosperity, peace and righteousness throughout Scripture (Mic. 4:4), and here indicate our basic human instinct for this fourfold blessing. God then chooses to clothe them himself, in recognition of fallen humanity's need for God's provision. Our own attempts at self-sufficiency fail to match God's provision.

Like the prodigal son, we find that despite our best intentions, without God's provision our plans lead us to bankruptcy. Yet, what a joy, the wandering son remembers his father and returns. To his great surprise his father is daily scanning the horizon in anticipation of his son's return (Luke 15:20). Hence, the robe and ring are ready and waiting, the calf fattened for the feast, and the vagrant's ragged garments are replaced. Clothed by God before their exile, Adam and Eve are dressed in the promise of God's future restoration and confirmation of Satan's defeat in seeking the destruction of God's created order. Today our need of clothing can act as a daily reminder of the forfeit of our original state with God and of the punishment for disobedience removed through Jesus who was stripped naked and died (Isa. 53:7) before being clothed in a glory initially unrecognisable to Mary at His resurrection (John 20:14–16).

SCRIPTURE TO CONSIDER: Ps. 30:6–12; Isa. 61:7–11; Luke 15:11–32; Rev. 19:11–21.

AN ACTION TO TAKE: Every day we rise from sleep and dress, so make this a time to give thanks to God and allow Him to clothe you in all you need to serve Him for the day ahead.

A PRAYER TO MAKE: 'Lord, since I have been raised with Christ through faith, may I daily put on garments of salvation and serve You. Amen.'

Romans 7:21–25

'For in my inner being I delight in God's law; but I see another law at work in me, waging war against the law of my mind and making me a prisoner of the law of sin at work within me.'(vv22–23)

A dam and Eve leave Eden in disobedience yet clothed in God's promise. The Garden wasn't evil, but they wilfully chose to violate God's instruction. Paul reflects their struggle, one common to us all. We must learn that we too live subject to the subtle temptations of God's enemy, Satan. There may be a strong desire to love and serve God and yet there's another irresistible drive towards things we know offend God. We too seek to disguise this aspect of ourselves, fearing exposure and rejection. Fearful we may succumb to Satan's charmed voice and like our first parents yield to what appears good and pleasing to the eye, and desirable for gaining wisdom (Gen. 3:6). Shame always follows rather than precedes our infringement. Throughout life we are at war with Satan, the consequences of which can damage us and hurt others. Sweet reason in various forms will attempt to excuse our disobedience, yet its fruit, separation from God, can only create the opportunity for us to turn against God. Discipleship is learning to choose God, doing whatever it takes to resist the 'law of sin' as it works to destroy us. Our futile attempts to hide from sin's reality only drags us deeper into Satan's clutches. We must look to God's Word and honest confession for our release from sin's icy grip. Selwyn Hughes described the Christian life as 'being trained in the knowledge of God's Word to overcome doubt and opposition and see God working in and through you to extend Christ's Kingdom'.*

SCRIPTURE TO CONSIDER: Eccl. 7:20–22; Rom. 7:1–20, 8:1–17; Jas 4:1–12.

AN ACTION TO TAKE: Read *Christ Empowered Living*, where Selwyn presents practical biblical insights to renew your mind and revolutionise your discipleship. Visit edwj.org/ja22-12aug

A PRAYER TO MAKE: 'Lord, who can rescue me from this body that is subject to death? Thank You that You deliver me through Jesus Christ our Lord! Amen.' (Rom. 7:24–25)

* Selwyn Hughes, *Cover to Cover Complete*, end of Section Four.

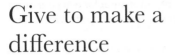

Give to make a difference

Our Bible reading notes are read by hundreds of thousands of people around the world. *Every Day with Jesus* and *Inspiring Women Every Day* are now free in the UK. We want everyone, whatever their financial means to have access to these resources that help them walk each day with our Saviour.

It makes all the difference. One reader in Malaysia said:

When I was first exposed to Every Day with Jesus about two years ago, I could sense something different, something refreshing, and I was energised. I used to struggle to translate knowledge into my daily life. EDWJ helped me to be more insightful, more positive, and to enjoy everyday life as a disciple. This helps me to be patient and positive at home, at work, and at church.

As we trust in God's provision, we know there are costs to providing this ministry. Can you give to make a difference in someone's life? Could supporting this vision be a way in which you serve?

A gift of just £2 a month from you will put daily Bible reading notes into the hands of at least one person who is hungry to know God and experience His presence every day.

Visit **wvly.org/donate** to give to make a difference, or use the form at the back of these notes.

Enemy at the Gate

Genesis 4:3–7
**'If you do what is right, will you not be accepted? But if
you do not do what is right, sin is crouching at your door;
it desires to have you, but you must rule over it.' (v7)**

The challenge we have with sin is that once we react inappropriately, as Cain did here in his anger with God in accepting Abel's and not his offering (v5), we open a door to a sin sequence with the potential for horrendous consequences. Once sin has a hold on our lives it seeks to sink us lower in the mire and it proves difficult to shake ourselves free and make our way back to God. The biblical image is stark: safe within our home whose walls and roof are constructed by God, step outside and a beast is waiting to pounce. We have friends in Montana, USA, who must be careful in the long winters to ensure there are no hungry bears roaming their property, ready to pounce upon a tasty lunch.

When we sin we are at serious risk of making a bad situation worse. We all too easily 'cut off our nose to spite our face', a needless action that vents anger but damages us more than whoever or whatever we are angry about. Sin becomes habitual unless we swiftly acknowledge we've sinned, confess to God and take a moment to reorientate ourselves. Like Joseph (Gen. 39:12) we are to flee from sin at the moment of its inception. Even when attracted by its promise, we are to resist, and the best way is like Joseph – to put some distance between ourselves and the source of our temptation. God knows and accepts our weakness, but do we?

SCRIPTURE TO CONSIDER: Gen. 39:1–20; Prov. 28:13–18; Matt. 26:36–46; 1 John 1:5–10.

AN ACTION TO TAKE: When temptation approaches you, like Joseph, what steps can you take to put some distance between you and the object of your desire? A practical process to adopt.

A PRAYER TO MAKE: 'Lord, You are my peace and I am safe within Your house. I look to You in times of temptation and trouble. Amen.'

2 Samuel 15:13–18
**'Then David said to all his officials who were with him in Jerusalem,
"Come! We must flee, or none of us will escape from Absalom.
We must leave immediately, or he will move quickly to overtake
us and bring ruin on us and put the city to the sword."' (v14)**

One constant challenge for Christians is when life takes a turn for the worse, no matter what we plan or do (2 Sam. 12:11). Within us there's a deeply rooted survival instinct. Despite our internet age someone has remarked, 'You can take the person out of the Stone Age, but you can't take the Stone Age out of the person.'* Consequently, we may act more from instinct than either reason or faith. Faith works on the basis of a trusted promise, whilst reason is a thought process by which a problem is identified, closely evaluated and then a solution chosen. Faith demands an active encounter with God, whilst reason requires a problem-solving brain. The former entrusts the outcome to God entirely, the latter waits with bated breath to see if the solution works. David's decision is instinctive. He knows God's promised to secure his lineage, but astutely appreciates that he must now leave Jerusalem to avoid disaster. Our life of discipleship has constantly moving parts within the overarching promises that nurture it. Therefore, there's a critical reason why we must learn to recognise God's voice and develop the sensitivity to respond as the Spirit leads. There's a danger that we may become insensitive to the gentle leading of God if we fail daily to deepen our connectedness with God. Discipleship is always growing our friendship with God, and this is the primary purpose for our life this side of eternity, and which will realise its fullest expression after death.

SCRIPTURE TO CONSIDER: 2 Sam. 19:9–23; Ps. 3:1–6; Matt. 11:1–18; Luke 11:33–36.

AN ACTION TO TAKE: Where and when do you take time to notice God's gentle leading? What impact has this had upon the shape your life has taken?

A PRAYER TO MAKE: 'Lord, You are my peace and I am safe within Your house. I look to You in times of temptation and trouble. Amen.'

* Nigel Nicholson, 'How Hardwired Is Human Behaviour?' (Harvard Business Review, July–August 1998).

2 Samuel 15:19–23
'But Ittai replied to the king, "As surely as the LORD lives, and
as my lord the king lives, wherever my lord the king may be,
whether it means life or death, there will your servant be."' (v21)

Absalom's rebellion begins, but Ittai, a Philistine, chooses to follow
David. When questioned why, Ittai responds that he'll follow the
king regardless of the cost, even if it means death. When the
Holy Spirit examines our choices and actions, what will they reveal
about our Christian faith? Will we be found to be following a false
king like Absalom? This rebel secured the love of David's subjects by
giving them what they wanted (2 Sam. 15:1–6). In return they gave their
loyalty so that they could secure the life they craved. Whilst it felt good,
it was a false substitute for the life and love of the true king. Being
comfortable and successful is no indication of God's favour.

David flees not from fear, but to ensure the city of God is not
devastated by Absalom's armed uprising (2 Sam: 15:14). We recall how
Mary, Joseph and Jesus were also forced to flee from Herod's sword
to protect God's promise. David fled to the wilderness, whilst they
hastened to Egypt. Severe disruption is something none of us relishes,
yet what price will we pay for peace, and a false peace at that? There
are times when I must leave my comfort zone to follow Christ faithfully,
and ensure that God's promise is not put to the sword. Paul confidently
asserts that nothing can separate us from God's love (Rom. 8:38–39).
How can I learn such confidence so that I, like Ittai, fearlessly follow
Jesus through every eventuality of life?

SCRIPTURE TO CONSIDER: 2 Sam. 18:1–18; Ruth 1:1–18; Matt. 2:13–18; Rom. 8:18–30.

AN ACTION TO TAKE: Be assured only God's promises are eternity proof. Are there issues that separate you from following God wholeheartedly?

A PRAYER TO MAKE: 'Lord, help me always to be prepared to go where You go, and stay where You stay. Amen.' (Ruth 1:16)

2 Corinthians 10:1–6
**'For though we live in the world, we do not wage war
as the world does. The weapons we fight with are not
the weapons of the world. On the contrary, they have
divine power to demolish strongholds.'(vv3–4)**

War is devastating, as that between Russia and Ukraine has
brought home to us all this year. Bertrand Russell, a lifetime
pacifist, wrote, 'Either Man will abolish war, or war will abolish
Man.'* It can prove controversial to adopt the language of warfare in
reference to our walk with God, yet Scripture makes it plain that we are
in the battle of our lives. Whilst assured that the final battle with Satan
is won through the death and resurrection of Jesus, we can become
unwittingly outmanoeuvred by the forces of Satan as they seek to make
incursions and disrupt our discipleship through attacking our supply
lines, preventing us from fulfilling God's call in our lives. This unseen
battle that seeks to fill the public square with proposals that demolish
the substance of our gospel are intended as far more than a simple
exchange of ideas. Any thought that we're continuously emerging from
a neanderthal battle for human survival through the development of
our intellectual understanding and our social refinement is Satan's
perennial attempt to blind the unbelievers (2 Cor. 4:4). Of course we
all struggle with disbelief in part, at which point the Christian disciple
is vulnerable to myopia at best, blindness at worst. There is a need to
recover an understanding of biblical cosmology and divine rule if we are
to stand any chance of collaborating in God's mission to make Christ
known to the ends of the earth (Acts 1:8) and prepare for His return.

SCRIPTURE TO CONSIDER: Gen. 3:13–15; Isa. 14:12–17; Luke 10:17–24; 1 Cor. 1:18–25.

AN ACTION TO TAKE: First we must understand our enemy, then we will need to
join the fight to demolish every stronghold that resists the will of God. Ready
for your marching orders?

A PRAYER TO MAKE: 'Lord, help me to take captive every thought and make it
obedient to Christ. Amen.' (2 Cor. 10:5)

* Bertrand Russell, *Fact and Fiction* (Unwin, 1961).

Spiritual Forces

Ephesians 6:10–18
'For our struggle is not against flesh and blood, but against the rulers, against the authorities, against the powers of this dark world and against the spiritual forces of evil in the heavenly realms.'(v12)

'That the devil has already been defeated and his kingdom laid waste – in the past tense for the New Testament authors – exposes him as little more than a raging beast, one with decidedly more bark than bite.'* Whilst the defeat of the counterfeit court of Satan is assured, the most that such principalities and powers can hope for is to usurp God's commitment to bring humanity to salvation. His weapons? Chaos, destruction arising from fear, in contrast to God's love. His planned assault on God (Isa. 14:13–15) failed when Jesus rose from the dead, depriving Satan of his authority over mortals, and gave Christ's followers the power to bind the strong man so that his possessions might be taken (Mark 3:23–27). Paul celebrates God's complete victory in Colossians: 'having disarmed the powers and authorities, he [Jesus] made a public spectacle of them, triumphing over them by the cross' (Col. 2:15).

So now the remnants of Satan's failed assault operate throughout the earth, with only one purpose: to whisper lies, as Satan did to Adam and Eve, in a vain hope of demoralising and drawing mortals away from God's rule. We are to be on full alert so that we might recognise the subtle deceit of these insurgents and ensure daily we put on God's provision for the fight of our lives by submitting ourselves to God, resisting the devil for he must then flee (Jas 4:7). Satan fights hard for he knows total obliteration is his final end (Rev. 12:12).

SCRIPTURE TO CONSIDER: Ezek. 28:11–19; Ps. 68:1–18; Col. 2:6–15; Heb. 2:14–18.

AN ACTION TO TAKE: What can you learn from the nature of this final cosmological battle between the outright purpose of God and Satan's misplaced attempt to supplant it?

A PRAYER TO MAKE: 'Lord, help me to fight the good fight knowing that You, the God of peace, will soon crush Satan under your feet. Amen.' (Rom. 16:20)

* Stepjen De Young, *The Religion of the Apostles* (Ancient Faith Publishing, 2021) p.83 Kindle.

Joshua 9:8–18
**'The Israelites sampled their provisions but did not enquire of the
LORD. Then Joshua made a treaty of peace with them to let them
live, and the leaders of the assembly ratified it by oath.' (vv14–15)**

It's clear that Christian life is demanding, and we do well to avoid
accepting Jesus' call casually. Choosing Jesus is to subscribe to
a worldview encompassing every aspect of reality, with helpful
guidance on how best to select our own activities. Gospel invitations
can be sugar-coated when expressing its many benefits (love, joy,
peace etc.), but Christianity isn't an off-the-shelf lifestyle but a custom-
made journey of exploration and discovery unique to each individual.
Its purpose is not to demonstrate God's existence – that is already
evident from creation (Rom. 1:20), through the ministry of Jesus and the
witness of God's Church – but to focus on journeying deeper into God's
heart and realising our ultimate value and purpose during our brief
mortal stay on earth. Our identity is in God and nowhere else.

It's easy to suffer lapses in judgment. The foundation module in
God's school of discipleship is how to remain focussed on God at
all times. We can quickly compartmentalise our lives. As we shut
our Bibles and conclude our formal prayers, we may unintentionally
close our hearts and minds to God's constant presence itself now
unrecognised (Luke 24:13–16). We quickly become invested in life's
worries, our anxiety leading us to poor decisions based on information
we haven't brought to God. I am all too familiar with this, and too often
I will live out of my emotional and intellectual reactions rather than
waiting upon God's counsel. Every mistake presents an opportunity to
learn and make improvement.

SCRIPTURE TO CONSIDER: 2 Sam. 21:2–6; Isa. 28:16–26; Rom. 2:1–9, 10:5–21.

AN ACTION TO TAKE: When you close your Bible do you keep the door to your
heart open for God's counsel?

A PRAYER TO MAKE: 'Lord, teach me to listen closely to You in every moment of
every day, and not take decisions without first talking with You. Amen.'

Psalm 19:7–9

'The precepts of the LORD are right, giving joy to the heart. The commands of the LORD are radiant, giving light to the eyes.' (v8)

A precept is a principle or rule, something that guarantees an outcome or a state of being. God's precepts offer us refreshment, confidence, wisdom, truth, joy, vision, clarity all of which outlast time itself and ensure that we reflect God's virtue, or so the psalmist declares! These characteristics are certainly ones I would want to be remembered by. It is by serving God with the entirety of ourselves that we access this treasure trove of human attributes. All that's required is that we take our stand upon God's promise entirely, and resist the many pressures that seek to persuade us to lower God's standards. Demanding of effort most certainly, but then every mountain is only scaled through premeditated effort. How much I want God will, as in all aspirations, depend upon the amount of perspiration I choose to invest.

As we have seen from Eden onwards, God places the decision squarely in our own hands. We may wrestle with all sorts of addictive behaviour, consistently fall foul of temptation, plumb the very depths of discouragement, yet God is neither disappointed in us nor critical of us. There will be consequences for those times when we fall from grace, but the joy of recovering our footing on the highway to heaven floods our whole being. Life progresses and there are key points at which we revise our focus and set off towards the horizon of hope born of the love and grace of God. Every time we refocus, our resolve to follow God grows stronger.

SCRIPTURE TO CONSIDER: Ps. 111:1–10; Zeph. 3:9–17; Rom. 5:6–21; 1 Tim. 6:2b–21.

AN ACTION TO TAKE: Take time to reflect upon the virtues presented in Psalm 19, and decide if these are worth making an effort to secure by God's grace.

A PRAYER TO MAKE: 'Lord, may the words of my mouth and this meditation of my heart be pleasing in Your sight, my Rock and my Redeemer. Amen.' (Ps. 19:14)

Matthew 22:34–40
'Jesus replied: "'Love the Lord your God with all your heart
and with all your soul and with all your mind.' This is the
first and greatest commandment. And the second is like
it: 'Love your neighbour as yourself.'"' (vv37–39)

Waverley Abbey is built on Jesus' summary of the Law and the
Prophets, teaching us to see everyone through Jesus' eyes.
There's no demand for anyone learning with us to have a faith-
based approach to life. Only that they recognise our understanding
grows from an ancient world view, evident throughout Scripture,
offering a realistic and comprehensive understanding of who we are,
why we're here, what's wrong with the world, and how this can be
addressed. Whilst only one amongst a number of approaches, it has
enjoyed the benefit of centuries of application and, whilst interpreted
through a variety of lenses, still addresses the critical questions of how
humans can creatively relate to life and each other.

For those of us who choose to build our life upon Christian precepts,
the whole weight of history and tradition places a responsibility for
action upon our shoulders. Jesus isn't arguing for mutual exchange.
At times we must grimly hang onto our love for God, despite contrary
evidence. Christianity is a tradition established and sustained by
faith (Heb. 11:1), faith in God's ability to fulfil His promise. It also
invites us to care for our neighbour (who is anyone we meet) without
expecting anything in return, because Christianity is established
through sacrificial initiatives, never built on the basis of transaction
or negotiation. Waverley Abbey believes that each of us can learn to
become the touchstone for positive and practical change in ourselves
and others, and so strengthen social cohesion through sacrificial love.

SCRIPTURE TO CONSIDER: Ps. 10:1–11; 2 Sam. 9:1–8; Luke 10:25–37; Heb. 11:8–16.

AN ACTION TO TAKE: God's heart is for us to be people who care and come
alongside one another. Read *Love with Skin On*. Visit edwj.org/ja22-20aug

A PRAYER TO MAKE: 'Lord, help me to become a practitioner of the two greatest
commandments You have given us. Amen.'

Beware

Romans 16:17–19
'For such people are not serving our Lord Christ, but their own appetites. By smooth talk and flattery they deceive the minds of naïve people.'(v18)

Maturity means developing our ability to make good choices. In our daily discipleship, we must beware of those factors that can slow, impede, even derail our commitment to God. This is not to raise our anxiety levels, for Paul makes it clear that we can draw reasonable assumptions from daily observations. The bedrock of our faith is obedience to God, but we find ourselves surrounded by many people offering 'valuable' advice on how best to live. As children we obediently followed the guidance of those caring for us, but as we mature and take increased responsibility for ourselves, we must learn decision making skills. Bad decisions usually lead to unhelpful consequences, yet we often only learn to make good decisions from our mistakes.

This methodology is one that easily translates to our Christian growth. God's grace is such that He knows we'll make bad decisions. However, God is always on hand to help us reflect on what a better decision might have been and how to move forward with our lives. Such reflection is sometimes done alone, often in conversation with trusted friends, and may be supported through the teaching programme of our church. Paul's concern is that there are some who appear to speak wisely, but who in fact are driven by their own agenda and want to navigate us away from God's grace and love. Always consider if your decisions reflect the character of God you discover in Scripture. God's Word is our life compass.

SCRIPTURE TO CONSIDER: Ps. 120; Jer. 9:1–9; Col. 2:1–8; 1 Pet. 3:8–22.

AN ACTION TO TAKE: How do you plan to get where you want to as a Christian? Set clear goals and target your energy and activities on maturing as a disciple.

A PRAYER TO MAKE: 'Lord, may I learn to make good decisions under the leadership of the Holy Spirit. Amen.' (1 John 2:27)

2 Timothy 1:6–9
**'For this reason I remind you to fan into flame the gift of
God, which is in you through the laying on of my hands.
For the Spirit God gave us does not make us timid, but
gives us power, love and self-discipline.'(vv6–7)**

O ne reason for bad decisions is the fact that we are often driven by our emotions. Someone once said, 'When angry we make the best speech we'll ever regret!' All of us can identify with the fiery and emotional speech we have made before spinning on our heels, leaving the room and slamming the door behind us. The immediate feelings of 'Well that told them!', slowly dissipate and we realise we now have to eat some humble pie and face the person we have wounded with our words. Not an easy point of re-entry, one that starts with an honest apology and proceeds from there. God is used to our repeated reactions and humble returns in search of His forgiveness, always immediately given.

A further skill that we develop through maturity is self-discipline or self-control. When we are encompassed in a red mist provoked by our emotions, best to press the pause button and place some distance between us and the object of our emotional excitement. Failure to do so can lead to conflict and behaviour that reflects our brokenness rather than God's grace. All disciplines are the fruit of commitment and practice. This is essential in learning to become self-disciplined. When we let our emotions control our actions, things quickly run away from us. We need to learn to analyse and manage our behaviour so that we cooperate with God in every circumstance. This will prove challenging, but serves as part of God's transformative purpose in our lives.

SCRIPTURE TO CONSIDER: 2 Chron. 15:1–9; Prov. 25:18–28; 1 Cor. 9:24–27; Col. 2:1–8.

AN ACTION TO TAKE: How good are you at identifying when you are being guided by your emotions rather than God's Spirit?

A PRAYER TO MAKE: 'Lord, help me to learn self-control through encounter with the Holy Spirit in every circumstance. Amen.'

Persist

James 1:2–8
'Because you know that the testing of your faith produces perseverance. Let perseverance finish its work so that you may be mature and complete, not lacking anything.'(vv3–4)

Perseverance acts as a prime motivator driving us both to attain our defined goals and to improve our skills. This drive is sustained by the passion we have for our goals and helps us to persist in our efforts, despite opposition and obstacles. It draws upon our motivation – how much we want something, and our determination, what we're prepared to spend on being successful. We know our human resolve is often weak. Most New Year resolutions are broken within hours! However, resolve is really the determination we decide to invest to accomplish something, even when we might remain unsure if and how we can accomplish it. This is a great description of the disciple's life. We set off in the direction of God, as if on a quest, and must overcome known and unknown challenges along the way. God has provided all the resources we need (1 Cor. 10:13), and it is always the intention that holds us to our course.

The Christian life is a marathon, not a sprint. We commit for the duration of our lives through all the many switchbacks we experience. One definition of madness is to keep doing the same thing repeatedly assuming you'll produce a different result. Perseverance requires reflection and creative thinking. If one strategy doesn't work, think, pray, talk with others, and find another. I once read on a tube train, 'Resolve is the fuel that drives the engine of accomplishment and you literally have an inexhaustible supply.' You alone have the power to shut it off.

SCRIPTURE TO CONSIDER: 1 Chron. 16:7–27; Ps. 37:23–29; Rom. 2:1–11; Heb. 10:32–39.

AN ACTION TO TAKE: What's the fuel that's driving your engine? Where is it taking you to? Is this your desired destination?

A PRAYER TO MAKE: 'Lord, may my perseverance build character and character sustain hope. So that I serve You faithfully every day. Amen.' (Rom. 5:3–4)

James 1:19–21

'My dear brothers and sisters, take note of this: everyone should be quick to listen, slow to speak and slow to become angry, because human anger does not produce the righteousness that God desires.' (vv19–20)

Training as a mediator I was reminded that I had two ears, but only one mouth; the moral being, listen twice as much as you speak. Good advice, but like many I have an opinion on everything and this remains a challenge. A study of Jesus' ministry reveals He asked many questions, and listened carefully to peoples' answers. He was interested in what lay behind the words, more than the words themselves. In listening we learn about the reasons why people are who they are, and express themselves in the way they do. This can constructively guide the nature of our response. Our desire is never about winning an argument but to encourage and enable others to discover the reality and value of the non-material in the context of our material perception and experience. Today, awash with virtual opinions, we swiftly 'Like' and forward soundbites born of style over substance. Our opinions twist and turn with the faintest of encouragement, and baying crowds quickly gather around a poorly conceived and only half considered piece of meaning. Learning to listen with respect to others' viewpoints, whilst reserving judgment, creates space in which understanding can be established through verbal exchanges. Agreement is never the objective, but showing the courtesy of listening demonstrates maturity, confidence in our perspective and an opportunity to advance knowledge to enrich everyone. Words spoken in haste, without thought, have mobilised armies and wreaked havoc throughout history. Language helps us build together; learning to live with disagreement is a positive consequence of our social experience.

SCRIPTURE TO CONSIDER: Prov. 12:13–23; Titus 3:1–11; Jas 3:1–12; 1 Pet. 3:8–17.

AN ACTION TO TAKE: What does having two ears and one mouth mean for you and how will this influence your interaction with others, face to face and on social media?

A PRAYER TO MAKE: 'Lord, may the words of my mouth and the thoughts of my heart; may the deeds of the day and the truth in my ways always speak of You. Amen.'*

Lyrics by Tim Hughes. Visit edwj.org/ja22-24aug [accessed 2022/04/03]

Hebrews 4:14–16
'Let us then approach God's throne of grace with confidence, so that we may receive mercy and find grace to help us in our time of need.' (v16)

Confidence is complete trust. We think about confidence in God (Jer. 17:7–8), but it's more challenging to place full confidence in ourselves. Jeremiah reminds us that confidence provides the roots to sustain us through uncertain seasons. Most often we act as our own harshest critic. God loves us despite knowing everything about us, but we never disillusion Him because He never had any illusions to start with. Step one in building our confidence is to accept ourselves as we are, just as God does. When we make comparisons with others, we are only judging ourselves through the lens of our own perception, and perceptions vary and never offer the whole truth.

We also build confidence through participating in peer groups. The purpose of church-based small groups is to support us through storytelling in discovering that each member, whilst different, has a unique and important contribution to make to the whole. Finally, it's good to set achievable challenges for ourselves to demonstrate we can complete our goals. Successfully reading *EDWJ* daily is one such challenge. These milestones help us to discover we can invest in achieving positive outcomes, rather than fretting at what we think we can't do. A great way to gain confidence is to do things that lie just outside of our natural comfort zone by entering the learning zone. Push too far, too fast and we enter the danger zone, and lose our confidence. Learning to love and serve God is a gradual and continuous movement outwards, which builds self-confidence along the way.

SCRIPTURE TO CONSIDER: Ps. 139:1–18; Isa. 41:8–13; Eph. 3:14–21; Phil. 1:3–11.

AN ACTION TO TAKE: How willing are you to move out of your comfort zone and explore the learning zone and all it offers in helping you to grow in self-confidence?

A PRAYER TO MAKE: 'Lord, search me and know my heart; test me and know my anxious thoughts. See if there is any offensive way in me, and lead me in the way everlasting. Amen.' (Ps. 139:23–24)

WAVERLEY ABBEY
COLLEGE

Did you know we have a Bradford Campus?

Church on the Way, Bradford, BD10 8SA

Develop your gifts | Be equipped | Make a difference

- Introduction to Christian Care and Counselling (ICCC)

- Diploma of Higher Education in Counselling

- Waverley Certificate in Christian Counselling

waverleyabbeycollege.ac.uk/bradford-campus

Take Ownership

Romans 8:28–31

'And we know that in all things God works for the good of those who love him, who have been called according to his purpose.' (v28)

There are two ways to look at our life experience. The one is to see things as happening to us, the other is to take ownership of them and then navigate our way through them. We can identify them as either threats or opportunities. Scripture encourages us to take hold of all our experiences and treat them as an opportunity. Paul, who pens these words, was no stranger to difficulties and it doesn't surprise us that his experience may well be ours. Our challenge is in taking ownership of our situation and so turning opposition and disappointment into good. Everything that we encounter can become a touchstone for deepening our encounter with God. We are called for God's purpose on earth, and it is up to us the degree to which we own and embrace that calling.

This is testing for us, for by comparison with what we had before, or in contrast with someone else's experience, it can seem as though we are hard done by. This of course brings God's reputation into consideration. Is His promise that everything works towards the ultimate realisation of excellence sufficient to enable us to own our mortal experiences and still give thanks to God? It goes to the very heart of our surrender to Jesus and the confidence we have in God's commitment never to fail or forsake us. It demands a counterintuitive approach, and reflects a world turned upside down (Acts 17:6, KJV). Can we own an inverted perspective?

SCRIPTURE TO CONSIDER: Gen. 50:15–21; Zech. 13:7–9; 2 Cor. 4:7–18, 11:16–33.

AN ACTION TO TAKE: How well are you able to embrace setbacks in your life and still hold on to God?

A PRAYER TO MAKE: 'Lord, help me to take ownership of each circumstance in my life and to hold fast to You whilst I am caught up in the storm. Amen.'

John 3:5–8
**The wind blows wherever it pleases. You hear its sound,
but you cannot tell where it comes from or where it is
going. So it is with everyone born of the Spirit.' (v8)**

The word 'listen' means both to hear and obey. Learning to discern God's voice from amongst the myriad sounds that surround us today is challenging. Of course listening is not simply through our ears. What we observe we may choose to copy, realising we have listened to a pattern for life. What we read we may take as our truth and so choose to disregard alternative perspectives. In other words, everything we encounter from the moment we wake to the time we drift off to sleep is a message that seeks to capture our attention and inform our understanding and behaviour. Such has become our fascination with fake news, that there are a host of fact checking websites, but of course how do I know I can trust them?

Jesus advises Nicodemus, a man in search of Truth that, like the wind, authenticity is difficult to establish both where it comes from and where it departs to. It is part of our Christian responsibility to learn how to take hold of God's truth. This is never formulaic but requires us to go in search of it within God's Word. Here we find a rich resource where we need the Spirit's insight to perceive beyond the obvious sense of the words on each page to discover the eternal and life-giving hope embedded within them. Like Nicodemus, truth can initially lie beyond rationality, and our job is tirelessly to search for God's way within God's Word.

SCRIPTURE TO CONSIDER: Ezek. 37:1–14; Eccl. 11:1–6; Mark 4:26–34; 1 Cor. 2:11–16.

AN ACTION TO TAKE: Where do you source your truth from? How do you decide between the many voices directed at you? Learn to listen to God's Spirit.

A PRAYER TO MAKE: 'Lord, guide me in my listening so that I can discern Your truth amongst the incessant noise created by so many voices directed at me. Amen.'

Be Positive

Psalm 103:1–6

'Praise the LORD, my soul, and forget not all his benefits – who forgives all your sins and heals all your diseases, who redeems your life from the pit and crowns you with love and compassion...'(vv2–4)

'**O**ur thoughts, emotions, and behaviours are all linked, so our thoughts impact how we feel and act. So, although we all have unhelpful thoughts from time to time, it's important to know what to do when they appear so we don't let them change the course of our day.'* This is the subtle way in which our thought patterns can shape our whole way of life. Many Christians say to me that they 'should' read their Bible or they 'ought' to pray more. Such language presents a trap. Neither should nor ought are quantifiable measures and therefore they tyrannise us with a sense of non-performance and failure. When it comes to both Bible reading and prayer, we set time aside, complete it and draw down the benefit of knowing we achieved what we set out to do. The objective is always to do things we can do, not live under the cloud of what we can't. As we mature we will begin to speak more positively. Having set a goal we will complete it and describe it positively; 'I read my Bible for fifteen minutes today', in contrast to some unattainable 'ought'. Positivity helps us get through difficult situations and overcome life's obstacles (Phil. 4:8). God is Himself positive and has revealed that everything ultimately ends positively. We may not always see this, but thinking that leads us to assume a fatal conclusion will increase our anxiety and increase our fear. We are to take every thought captive (2 Cor. 10:5)!

SCRIPTURE TO CONSIDER: Jer. 29:4–23; Ps. 18:1–36; Rom. 10:5–13; Rev. 11:15–19.

AN ACTION TO TAKE: Observe your thoughts and ask yourself if it's helpful? How does it serve you? How does it make you feel? Then turn it into a positive one.

A PRAYER TO MAKE: 'Lord, help me to take every thought captive and grow the mind of Christ within me. Amen.' (1 Cor. 2:16)

* Rachel Goldman, PhD, a psychologist and clinical assistant professor at the NYU School of Medicine.

John 15:9–17

'My command is this: love each other as I have loved you. Greater love has no one than this: to lay down one's life for one's friends. You are my friends if you do what command.' (vv12–14)

O ur focus has been on pursuing God's purpose in our lives. According to British researchers Andrew Steptoe and Daisy Fancourt, 'Maintaining a sense that life is worthwhile may be particularly important at older ages when social and emotional ties often fragment, social engagement is reduced, and health problems may limit personal options.'* As youthful enthusiasm abandons us to ageing, we focus more on life's purpose. We must consider if the pleasure principle (our instinctive search for pleasure and avoiding pain for immediate gratification) is sufficient. A mature faith draws comfort from the implicit delayed gratification in Jesus' promise of an eternal future, for which we have been created. Part of that process may well be making personal sacrifices on behalf of others. Perhaps as parents we'll instinctively make sacrifices for our children, but that is not a given. Jesus demonstrated what sacrifice looks like, and it's not initially an appealing vision. However, on further consideration, to lay a life down for the benefit of humanity is a noble purpose, and one which we can all learn from. A sign of maturity is being responsible enough to make sacrifices for the good of others and the future without any resentment. Responsible people understand that sometimes gratification needs to be delayed now in order to attain a future outcome. Delayed gratification requires learning how to manage our present need for satisfaction through an anticipation of how it enables us to thrive. Over time, delaying gratification will improve our self-control and help bring focus to our long-term goals.

SCRIPTURE TO CONSIDER: Gen. 25:29–34; 1 Sam. 24:1–7; Matt. 16:21–28; Heb. 6:12–20.

AN ACTION TO TAKE: How do you consider the pleasure principle in the decisions you make? Are you able to patiently live in anticipation of God's promise?

A PRAYER TO MAKE: 'Lord, my heart yearns for You; my heart and my flesh cry out for the living God. Amen.' (Ps. 84:2)

Give Back

Luke 6:37–42

'Give, and it will be given to you. A good measure, pressed down, shaken together and running over, will be poured into your lap. For with the measure you use, it will be measured to you.'(v38)

Researchers from the University of Nottingham in England set out to answer the question: Are people who practice gratitude more likely to help others, share, volunteer and donate?* They found a clear link between gratitude and behaviour that helps society as a whole. Also, individuals with a broader outlook of gratitude and appreciation of the positive in the world proved more likely to engage in helping others compared with those for whom gratitude is a passing emotion. It appears that a positive outlook and generosity of heart benefits others whilst also providing the giver with protection against stress. Giving back isn't necessarily financial but can be expressed with our time, knowledge, and personal engagement. For example, since launching in 1976, Habitat for Humanity has helped over 29 million people improve their housing conditions and start independent lives with support from volunteers and partners. Giving back demonstrates that we have shifted our focus from ourselves and, like Jesus, are looking to the interests of others. In a world often presented as selfish, and with many people dealing with anxiety due to isolation, reaching out, giving back and attempting to build community creates a space within which the character of God can be expressed. Just as Jesus gave up the security of heaven to live on earth, so we can move our focus from concerns just about our own welfare and seek to give back from all that we have received by grace already (Matt. 10:7–8).

SCRIPTURE TO CONSIDER: Prov. 19:16–23; Hos. 2:14–23; Matt. 5:43–48; 2 Cor. 9:6–14.

AN ACTION TO TAKE: Are you ready to shift your focus from yourself to others? What will this mean in practice?

A PRAYER TO MAKE: 'Lord, help me to be one who builds community through giving back as a sign of the kingdom of God on earth. Amen.'

* edwj.org/ja22-30aug [accessed 2022/04/05]

Psalm 16:5–8
'I will praise the LORD, who counsels me; even at night my heart instructs me. I keep my eyes always on the LORD. With him at my right hand, I shall not be shaken.' (vv7–8)

The foundational message that runs through all of Scripture is that God is for each one of us. How we respond to that knowledge is a matter of personal choice, and any survey would reveal that individuals are at different stages of their acceptance of God, and in the degree to which they are comfortable entrusting God with their wellbeing, even with His many witnesses throughout our material world (Rom. 1:20). One essential message in all of Scripture is that God is all sufficient and in Him we can find the fullest expression of who we have been created to be. We also gain insight into who it is we might become by God's grace.

It is a challenging choice which faces us, as one day gives way to the next to determine the level of excitement and devotion we will invest in God's promise in living God's way in God's world. Satan constantly seeks to undermine our confidence in God, directly and indirectly. One way I deal with this when struggling is to ask myself what are the alternatives? There may be a number, but the majority of them whilst perhaps offering a quick fix or immediate release of my tension, carry no hope for my future. God's light is perhaps best seen in the context of the darkness which it attempts to illuminate and will ultimately overcome. When I am determined always to keep my eyes on God then I am indeed looking to the light that can sustain me against all odds.

SCRIPTURE TO CONSIDER: Ps. 78:40–56; Lam. 3:19–33; Matt. 6:19–24; 1 Pet. 4:1–11.

AN ACTION TO TAKE: What are the things that jostle in your heart and mind to disrupt your friendship with God, and what will it take for you to declare, 'Apart from God I have nothing'?

A PRAYER TO MAKE: 'Lord, please make known to me the path of life; fill me with joy in your presence. Amen.' (Ps. 16:11).

Notes

Order form

Get Your **FREE** Daily Bible Reading Notes **TODAY!** (UK ONLY)

Your favourite Bible Reading notes are now available to you for FREE. God has called us back to the original vision of CWR to provide these notes to everyone who needs them, regardless of their circumstance or ability to pay. It is our desire to see these daily Bible reading notes used more widely, to see Christians grow in their relationship with Jesus on a daily basis and to see Him reflected in their everyday living. Clearly there are costs to provide this ministry and we are trusting in God's provision.

Could you be part of this vision? Do you have the desire to see lives transformed through a relationship with Jesus? **A small donation from you of just £2 a month, by direct debit, will make such a difference** Giving hope to someone in desperate need whilst you too grow deeper in your own relationship with Jesus.

4 Easy Ways To Order

1. Visit our online store at **waverleyabbeyresources.org/store**
2. Send this form together with your payment to:
   CWR, Waverley Abbey House, Waverley Lane, Farnham, Surrey GU9 8EP
3. Phone in your credit card order: **01252 784700** (Mon–Fri, 9.30am – 4.30pm)
4. Visit a Christian bookshop

For a list of our National Distributors, who supply countries outside the UK, visit waverleyabbeyresources.org/distributors

Your Details (required for orders and donations)

Full Name: CWR ID No. (if known):

Home Address:

                                              Postcode:

Telephone No. (for queries):   Email:

Publications

TITLE	QTY	PRICE	TOTAL
Total Publications			

UK P&P: up to £24.99 = **£2.99**; £25.00 and over = **FREE**

Elsewhere P&P: up to £10 = **£4.95**; £10.01 – £50 = **£6.95**; £50.01 – £99.99 = **£10**; £100 and over = **£30**

Total Publications and P&P (please allow 14 days for delivery)   **A**

Payment Details

☐ I enclose a cheque made payable to CWR for the amount of: **£**

☐ Please charge my credit/debit card.

Cardholder's Name (in BLOCK CAPITALS) _____

Card No. ☐☐☐☐ ☐☐☐☐ ☐☐☐☐ ☐☐☐☐ ☐☐☐☐

Expires End ☐☐ ☐☐   Security Code ☐☐☐

Continued overleaf >>

<< See previous page for start of order form

One off Special Gift to CWR ☐ Please send me an acknowledgement of my gift **B**

GRAND TOTAL (Total of A & B)

Gift Aid (your home address required, see overleaf)

giftaid it I am a UK taxpayer and want CWR to reclaim the tax on all my donations for the four years prior to this year and on all donations I make from the date of this Gift Aid declaration until further notice.*

Taxpayer's Full Name (in BLOCK CAPITALS) _____

Signature _____ **Date** _____

*I am a UK taxpayer and understand that if I pay less Income Tax and/or Capital Gains Tax than the amount of Gift Aid claimed on all my donations in that tax year it is my responsibility to pay any difference.

Your FREE Daily Bible Reading Notes Order

	Please Tick	FREE	£2 pcm	£5 pcm	£10 pcm	Other
Every Day with Jesus (1yr, 6 issues)		☐	☐	☐	☐	☐ £ ___
Large Print *Every Day with Jesus* (1yr, 6 issues)		☐	☐	☐	☐	☐ £ ___
Inspiring Women Every Day (1yr, 6 issues)		☐	☐	☐	☐	☐ £ ___

All CWR Bible reading notes are also available in single issue **ebook** and **email subscription** format. Visit **waverleyabbeyresources.org** for further info

---

CWR Instruction to your Bank or Building Society to pay by Direct Debit
Please fill in the form and send to: CWR, Waverley Abbey House,
Waverley Lane, Farnham, Surrey GU9 8EP

DIRECT Debit

Name and full postal address of your Bank or Building Society

To: The Manager _____ Bank/Building Society

Address _____

_____

_____ Postcode

Name(s) of Account Holder(s)

Branch Sort Code

Bank/Building Society Account Number

Originator's Identification Number

4	2	0	4	8	7

Reference

Instruction to your Bank or Building Society

Please pay CWR Direct Debits from the account detailed in this Instru
subject to the safeguards assured by the Direct Debit Guarantee. I
understand that this Instruction may remain with CWR and, if so, det
will be passed electronically to my Bank/Building Society.

Signature(s)

_____

Date

Banks and Building Societies may not accept Direct Debit Instructions for some types of account

---

**For a subscription outside of the UK please visit www.waverleyabbeyresources.or
where you will find a list of our national distributors.**

How would you like to hear from us? We would love to keep you up to date on all aspects of the CWR ministry,
ding; new publications, events & courses as well as how you can support us.

DO want to hear from us on email, please tick here [ ] If you **DO NOT** want us to contact you by post, please tick he
update your preferences at any time by contacting our customer services team on 01252 784 700. You can view our privacy policy online at waverleyabbeyresources.org